TO BE A PILOT

The story of a Liverpool Marine Pilot

David Devey

Grosvenor House
Publishing Limited

All rights reserved
Copyright © David Devey, 2024

The right of David Devey to be identified as the author of this
work has been asserted in accordance with Section 78
of the Copyright, Designs and Patents Act 1988

The book cover is copyright to David Devey

This book is published by
Grosvenor House Publishing Ltd
Link House
140 The Broadway, Tolworth, Surrey, KT6 7HT.
www.grosvenorhousepublishing.co.uk

This book is sold subject to the conditions that it shall not, by way of
trade or otherwise, be lent, resold, hired out or otherwise circulated
without the author's or publisher's prior consent in any form of
binding or cover other than that in which it is published and
without a similar condition including this condition being
imposed on the subsequent purchaser.

A CIP record for this book
is available from the British Library

Paperback ISBN 978-1-80381-898-6
Hardback ISBN 978-1-80381-899-3
eBook ISBN 978-1-80381-900-6

LIST OF CHAPTER SUBJECTS

PREFACE	v
PROLOGUE	xi
CHAPTER ONE: GROWING UP	1
CHAPTER TWO: SEA CADETS	8
CHAPTER THREE: SEATIME	14
CHAPTER FOUR: LIFE AS A BOATHAND	32
CHAPTER FIVE: LIFE AS A THIRD CLASS PILOT	49
CHAPTER SIX: LIFE AS A SECOND CLASS PILOT	57
CHAPTER SEVEN: LIFE AS A FIRST CLASS PILOT	63
CHAPTER EIGHT: LIFE IN THE REPUBLIC OF GUINEA	67
CHAPTER NINE: RETURN TO LIVERPOOL	78
CHAPTER TEN: LIFE AS AN EMPLOYEE	83
CHAPTER ELEVEN: THE BATTLE FOR FREEDOM	87
CHAPTER TWELVE: DELIVERENCE	100
CHAPTER THIRTEEN: RETURN TO SELF-EMPLOYMENT	105
CHAPTER FOURTEEN: RETIREMENT AND VINDICATION	116

PREFACE

This book is about marine pilots, and not the airline variety, so if you are feeling disappointed, please return it to the top shelf and maybe look under the heading "Biggles".

The pilots I am talking about were on this planet long before our illustrious counterparts in the sky, and as a body of men, tend to shun publicity in the performance of their daily duties. As a result, the vast majority of the general public have no conception of what a pilot actually does, and this book sets out to fill in those gaps in knowledge that currently exist.

If you are still reading this, and haven't returned it to the top shelf, then welcome aboard! In this book, you will read what actually happens in the life of a marine pilot. It is written by a man who spent his whole working life in pilotage - from being an apprentice at 16 years of age, to completing 40 years of service as a licensed/ authorised pilot, and duly retiring at age 65. This period included a secondment of 2 years away from my home port of Liverpool and spent in the Republic of Guinea at Port Kamsar, of which I will speak in a later chapter. In those 40 years, I came very near to meeting my maker on no less than 3 occasions, once as an apprentice and twice as a licensed pilot, but each time my guardian angel stepped in at the eleventh hour to rescue me from my fate.

One of the principal reasons for me writing this book is to express my grave concerns over the lack of recognition by successive British governments, both Tory and Labour, of the importance of the role of the marine pilot in this island nation of ours. Over 90% of all goods imported to and exported from the UK are transported by ship. Most of these ships, especially the larger ones, are guided in and out of our ports by authorised pilots. As a former licenced, and later authorised pilot for the Port of Liverpool, with over 40 years' experience of handling ships of all sizes, from the smallest coaster to the largest passenger liner, and having retired with an accident-free record, I feel it my duty to bring this unhappy position to the attention of the great British public. One of the reasons for the existence of this unfortunate situation rests with the pilots themselves, who are notoriously shy in promoting what they do, and as a consequence, most members of the public are unaware that pilots even exist, and if they do know of their existence, quite often they do not know just what a pilot does. On the occasions when I have been asked "What did you do for a living?", I have always been careful to reply with the words "*Marine* pilot", as otherwise the next question is "Which airline did you fly with?". Then, when corrected that I was a ship's pilot, the next question invariably is "Oh, are you the man who goes out on the tugboat then?" Answer "No. I go on board the ship." "Well, how do you get on board the ship then?" And so on…

The lack of knowledge as to what a pilot does is another reason for me writing this book, and it is to educate the public, both in what a pilot does, and more importantly, what his responsibilities are when on duty. The common public misconception is that the pilot is merely an adviser and that it is the captain who actually brings his ship into and out of port. This could not be further from the truth and, in particular at my home port of Liverpool, where the spring tides can rise and fall more than 10 metres twice daily.

An authorised pilot acting in UK waters is subject to an act of parliament (currently the '1987 Pilotage Act'), and under its articles he can be fined or sent to prison for his actions whilst on board ship. He is not an adviser, but very much a 'hands on' person who takes the charge of the navigation of the vessel, following an introductory exchange of information with the ship's master. His duties include the directing of the course in which the ship will proceed, the speed at which the ship will travel, a careful appraisal of the underwater clearance of the vessel (due to the rise and fall of tide), and continuous radio contact with the shore-based port control operatives, the tugs that will make fast to the ship, and other vessels navigating at the same time. All in all, a very busy and complex procedure which is further complicated when the vessel is approaching the harbour. This is when the assisting tugs will need to be made fast to the vessel, and subsequently directed by the pilot's radio as to when and where to give assistance in helping the vessel to dock safely. Only when the vessel is safely moored and out of any danger, is the pilot's task finished. Add to these factors the different weather conditions a pilot might experience (for example strong winds and night-time operations), and of course thick fog which can descend very quickly and sometimes at crucial points in the navigation, and you have a small idea of the responsibilities of the modern-day pilot. I did however forget to mention one other factor, and that of course is the condition of the vessels themselves being piloted, and the competence of their diverse crews of different nationalities. There is nothing more daunting to a pilot when he is approaching a concrete quay head-on and having ordered the engines to go astern (backwards) in order to stop the ship from colliding with the dock wall, to be informed by the master that the engines are no longer working… I had this experience a few times myself in the course of my career, and on one occasion, when on board an old Greek vessel, approaching the dock wall at Birkenhead. I asked for "half astern" (half speed backwards) on the engines and nothing happened. We were getting ever nearer to impact when I asked for "full astern" (full speed backwards). Seconds went by before finally the engine spluttered into life, and even then, the performance was pathetic… I gripped the handrail, bracing myself for the inevitable crash and the banshee-like wailing of the sound of steel coming into contact with concrete, when miraculously the ship stopped inches short of the quay! When I asked the Greek master why the stern power of the vessel was so poor, he replied with a big smile full of gold-teeth, and in a typically Greek way shrugging his shoulders, "Sorry mister pilot, but we don't make any money going astern." To compensate for giving me such a fright he thrust a bottle of Johnny Walker Red Label whisky into my bag (which was the standard Greek practice for soothing a pilot's nerves following severe fright) and it also served as an encouragement to try that little bit harder to make sure that his ship finished the voyage in one piece.

If you are still interested to know what it is like to be a pilot, then read on… Incidentally if you are still reading at this late stage, you might attract some funny stares from the bookseller who is by now wondering if you do intend to make a purchase. In this book, I have thrown in some funny anecdotes, and I describe some of the characters that I have met and worked with in the forty years I have spent as a river pilot for the Port of Liverpool. I hope that at the end of it, you may have a better understanding of what it's like to be a pilot both in the UK - and every other country in the world, as the marine pilotage profession is universal.

DAVID DEVEY
30. 10. 2021

David Devey passed away on 16th January 2022 aged 80 years old.

He is sorely missed by his family and friends.

PROLOGUE

This book is dedicated to all pilots world-wide, both serving and retired. You alone know what being a pilot involves - the huge burden of responsibility that goes with the profession, of having to make on-the-spot decisions, which if wrong, could cost the lives of numerous individuals, to say nothing of the millions of pounds created by any damage and the resulting pollution. You alone know the feeling of loneliness that can go with the isolation of being the only person on board ship who is capable of making those crucially important decisions, with no one to consult for advice, but relying solely on your own judgement. You alone know those times when everything seems stacked against you with a rusting ship, the visibility down to zero with a poor radar set, and with only enough air in the cylinders for one more engine start. The problems that a pilot has to face are numerous and complex, and sadly, all too many shore-based people either do not understand what they face on a daily basis, or worse than that, do know, and yet still choose to degrade the profession. As a pilot myself with 40 years' experience and having come close to losing my life on no less than 3 occasions in my working time, I feel particularly aggrieved by the attitude of successive UK governments towards the pilotage profession. Considering the UK is an island nation that depends on the sea and its ports for 90% of its trade, the importance of the very people whose skills keep 'the show on the road' is almost entirely overlooked.

CHAPTER ONE: GROWING UP

I was born and raised in Tranmere, a suburb of Birkenhead, nestling on the banks of the River Mersey. Our house was part of a typical two-up two-down development built for the workers of the nearby shipyard 'Cammell Lairds', and each house had its own outdoor toilet situated at the end of the back yard, with a walled enclosure where the coal bunker stood along. Heating for the entire house was care of a coal fire in the living room, of which it was my duty at an early age to light each evening before the return of my mother from her workplace at the Stork Margarine factory at nearby Bromborough village. It was in this house that I spent the formative years of my life along with my brother Don who was 2 years older than me, and my elder brother Eric who was a ship's carpenter working at sea with the Blue Funnel Line. This shipping company had its headquarters in Liverpool and operated a fleet of over 90 vessels which traded to the far east including Japan, China, Malaysia, and Indonesia. I was later to spend nearly 2 years as a cadet with this company where I fell in love with the oriental mystique of Hong Kong, our Far East terminal. But all that is for later.

In my infancy I attended the nursery on Dacre Hill along with my brother Don, and each day we would travel by bus and be dropped off by my mother on her way to work, and each evening she would pick us up to bring us back home. The staff at the nursery were very caring and it was a happy period in my life (what I can remember of it at that early age). The fire lighting came much later when I became part of the real world of growing up!

The local primary school was Well Lane, though I never did see any sign of a well in the locality. The school was staffed by blown-away Scottish ladies, most of whom were old maids, and all of them seemed to spend their lives reminiscing about their beloved homeland of Scotland. As a result, I was brought up able to sing most of the Scottish folksongs and my knowledge of Gaelic was infinitely better than that of

English, though I never did find out what "Many a mickle makes a muckle" meant. I'm still no wiser now! Well Lane was a mixed primary school where I first came into contact with those strange creatures called *girls*. They played their own games of skipping and netball whilst we lads kicked a tennis ball around the school yard until the bell went for classes. They were forever reporting us to the duty teacher for alleged misbehaviour and soon earned the nickname of "clat tale tits" from us boys.

Dave Devey (left) with his brother Don (right).

The girls had a saying at the time which went "What are little boys made of?" with the answer "Slugs and snails and puppy-dogs' tails" (I suppose that last bit was appropriate!) and then went "What are little girls made of?" with the answer "Sugar and spice and all things nice." In those days boys and girls did not mix too well. In my fourth year at Well Lane, I was made a prefect whose principal job was to man the school gate on the sound of the teacher's hand bell indicating nine o'clock and the start of classes. Invariably, the same characters turned up late every morning in the tow of an irate mother who would plead with me to let their little darling in so as not to be marked as late. The most frequent offender was a lad called Arthur Quigly, who went on in later life to murder a local vagrant for which he was jailed for 15 years. I still wonder to this day whether his antagonism towards society had its early development in my steadfast refusal to allow him through the school gate... My term of office as prefect was short-lived however, as I was reported by a local resident whose house overlooked the school for shinning up a drainpipe and climbing onto the school roof looking for lost tennis balls after school hours. I was publicly stripped of my badge of office and my arch-nemesis Frank Hadfield who was a 'goody goody' (someone who never did anything wrong) was installed in my place. That may well have been the beginning of my rebellious nature which went on throughout my life and still continues to this day.

My four year stay at Well Lane came to an end in late 1952 when I gained a scholarship to Birkenhead School. In a way I was lucky in the exam as one of the tests was a recognition of a photograph printed in the Liverpool Echo at the time, which depicted policemen out of uniform with arms linked together practicing crowd control for the future Queen Elizabeth's forthcoming coronation. Why I say I was lucky was down to my daily task of lighting the lounge fire in the evening. Because we could not afford to buy the ready-made bundles of sticks that were on sale at the local corner shop which were used along with paper to ignite the coal, I was obliged to roll up sheets of newspaper in order to replicate the sticks of wood. In the course of doing this, I would sometimes read the newspaper which the kind old lady next door Mrs. Jackson gave to us when she had finished reading it. One day whilst lighting the fire, I had seen the very same picture and read through the article prior to screwing it up and burning it. Thus, in the interview I was able to identify exactly what the people in it were doing which, without seeing that article first-hand, would have been difficult, if not impossible. Lady luck was on my side that day. I still feel to this day that that was the clincher that tipped the scales in favour of my passing the exam. I was painfully aware that if I did not succeed in that exam, I would not be able to go to the fee-paying public school which was well beyond the means of my mother who was employed as a cook at the Bromborough factory and earning only £6 per week supplemented only by her widow's pension, Birkenhead School is a northern public school situated in the leafy area of Oxton, a suburb of the town of Birkenhead which came to prominence with the introduction of shipbuilding by a

Dave Devey (left) with his brother Don (right).

Scotsman called John Laird and which later became known as Cammell Lairds. At that time the vast majority of its pupils came from middle class families who were able to afford the annual fees, but governmental changes brought about the possibility of pupils being able to enter on a free scholarship basis. My brother Don and I both gained entry through this system. It represented a big change in my life as I was no longer a big fish in a small pond but was now swimming in a large pond with fish who were often a lot cleverer than me and, in most cases, better endowed (financially I mean!). It was a time of adapting to the new circumstances which I quickly did and my first two years in junior school were happy ones although my predilection for mischief occasionally got me into hot water which would result in 6 strokes of the cane from the junior school headmaster Mr. (Daddy) Rankin. He was a leading light in The Church of Scientology and seemed to enjoy the task of beating young boys on the pretext that this would hurt him more than it would hurt them. I would have liked to have seen the roles reversed to test as to whether this opinion could be true but sadly, I was never offered the chance. It was at this time that my brother Don and I went on a cycling holiday to London and the Isle of Wight using the local youth hostels. This was to instil in me a deep love of the English countryside which is still with me to this day. It was 1955 and a time when there were no motorways - just A roads - which took you through the most beautiful countryside and into the middle of quaint towns and villages where people spoke with differing accents the further south you travelled. However, the journey wasn't without its problems and not a few hardships. The other participants were all friends of my brother who had organised the trip and were therefore two years older than me and all had lightweight racing bikes with multiple gears. My bike was a standard Raleigh Roadster with no gears for assistance which became my handicap for the full two weeks that we were on the road. Our first overnight stop was the youth hostel at Ludlow, a distance of some 80 miles from our starting point in Tranmere. The main road was the A41 which took us to Chester and then on to Whitchurch where we followed the A49 signposted for Shrewsbury and ultimately on to Ludlow. What I hadn't anticipated was that the others in the party including my brother would race off ahead and leave me pedalling away on my own for the whole of the trip. For a 14-year-old without any kind of a map - or even a road atlas - it was a daunting experience as I had previously never been further than a visit to my uncle Eric who lived in the Huyton district of Liverpool and that was courtesy of the 6A tram from the Liverpool Pierhead. So, the die was cast, and it soon became my realisation that every morning after completing the tasks given to each member by the warden of the youth hostel, I would be told the name of the next destination and then left to find my own way there. Time to grow up-and fast! Talking about wardens, I had an unpleasant experience with one during the trip when I accidently dropped a piece of paper when pulling out my youth hostel card which had to be deposited on arrival before being stamped with the logo of that place prior to being returned the next morning. The irate warden proceeded to give me a stern lecture on the polluting aspects of discarded litter before I had a chance to protest that I had not done it deliberately, as I also hate litter myself, and on picking up my card the next morning I found that he had firmly pasted a "Keep Britain Tidy" sticker onto the inside of my card where it still stands to this day. Some of the wardens who ran the youth hostels in those days were complete tyrants in their behaviour towards travellers. A lot were ex-military and ran the place like an army barracks. They even had the power to confiscate a person's card which denied him access to any other youth hostel that he may have planned to visit, so it was in everybody's interest not to cross them. Having said that, the vast majority of youth hostels were pleasant places to stay, and travellers were usually tired and ready for bed soon after supper. It certainly was the case for me, as I would arrive some many hours after the others and often after dark, and just in time for a bite to eat and off to bed in readiness for the next day's ride. The route took us through Worcester, the beautiful vale of Evesham, and on to our next stop at Stow-on-the-Wold in Gloucester. As I said before, this trip opened my eyes to the beauty of the English countryside, and it was here that I first tasted that phenomenal experience in the counties of Hereford, Worcester, and Gloucester. Today, with all the motorways that now exist, and people who are only interested in getting to their destination as soon as possible, this incredible beauty is all too often missed.

Our journey took us on via a small village called Jordans to the youth hostel at Earls Court in London where we spent 3 days taking in the sights of the capital which, to a youngster of some 14 years, were somewhat awe inspiring. It was also a chance for me to recover from the four days of non-stop cycling which had preceded our arrival, so the break for me was most welcoming. However, it was too short-lived, and we were once more on the road this time on the A3 and heading for the Isle Of Wight. This proved to be the most arduous part of the journey as our next youth hostel booking was on the island itself and we needed to make the ferry connection from Gosport across to the island, before we could make the final ride to the youth hostel at Medham House, in Cowes. This we had to do in one day and it pushed me to the limits of my endurance, especially as I was riding a basic bike with no gears for assistance and having to find my way through London, before setting off on the A3 and arriving at the ferry terminal in sufficient time for the last ferry across. I think my guardian angel worked overtime that day, and I managed to survive the ordeal and joined the others at the ferry terminal to the Isle Of Wight just in time for the last boat. That was one of the occasions where I cried to myself out of sight of the others, mostly through relief of having made the ferry. I did not want any of the others to think that I wasn't up to it and besides, it would have been reported back to the school and damaged my standing with my fellow pupils…

We spent two days on the island cycling round to the south coast from east to west passing through Ventnor and on to the hostel at Whitwell. From there on up the west coast to Yarmouth where we joined the ferry bound to Lymington on the mainland. We were now on the homeward leg and heading west picking up the A35 and into the beautiful county of Dorset and to Bridport where we spent the night. Then to the ferry crossing of the Severn over to Chepstow (readers will note that the Severn Bridge did not exist then). I was now beginning to feel that I might actually complete this herculean task and so I steeled myself for the problems that lay ahead. From Chepstow, we followed the beautiful River Wye all the way north to a small village called Welsh Bicknor where the youth hostel was situated. The river served as the border between England and Wales and on the other bank was English Bicknor. I remember it was raining heavily the following morning as we were getting ready to leave and the baker had arrived with a large tray of bread which he had balanced on his head. He was delivering the daily supply of bread from English Bicknor to the youth hostel at Welsh Bicknor, and this involved him having to paddle across the ford between the two villages. Unfortunately, whilst negotiating the now treacherous grass bank down to the river he lost his footing and the tray of bread ended up in the river. So, no bread for breakfast that morning. Looking back on the whole trip many years later, I came to the conclusion that this was the most beautiful part of Britain that I have ever visited, both before and ever after.

On our return journey through the beautiful county of Worcester we passed the signpost for the village of Mamble, made famous by the poet John Drinkwater, who imagined what the place would look like with such a lazy sounding name and contemplates whether he should take the road and see for himself, but ultimately decides not to go in case he is disappointed with what he finds.

Then onwards to Shrewsbury for the night, and then the final leg home on the A41 through Whitchurch and the rolling plains of Cheshire and back to the realities of life as a 14-year-old in Tranmere. But that experience of rural England was to stay with me for the rest of my life and helped to mould me as a dyed-in-the-wool Brit. I still haven't found anywhere to match that charm and beauty that emanates from the English countryside having traversed the globe in the years that followed.

CHAPTER TWO: SEA CADETS

I remember as a boy those occasional trips across the Mersey on the ferry now made famous by the Gerry Marsden's song "Ferry Cross the Mersey". The cost then was one penny in the old currency and the trick was to hide in the toilets when the ferry tied up at Liverpool and stay on board for the return trip. You could spend the day there for just the price of one trip and imagine that you were at sea with all the sounds and smells of an ocean-going liner. Those ferry trips helped spark my interest in a nautical career and prompted me to join the local sea cadet corps of T.S. Seahawk based in Bebington, a town close to Birkenhead. Seahawk was commanded by a former Liverpool pilot apprentice who lost the sight in one eye in a firework accident and was forced to give up his career as a Liverpool Pilot. The reader may begin to see the connections leading up to my chosen career from this information and he would be right, as I had set my mind on becoming a Liverpool Pilot following my enlistment in the sea cadets under the tutelage of Lieutenant Commander Arkell. Ken Arkell was a very likeable man who early on adopted a policy of helping youths who had fallen foul of the law, and he had come to an arrangement with the local magistrate to accept as cadets certain boys who they thought could be helped as an alternative to a spell in the correction centre known as borstal. To his great credit the names of those boys was always kept a secret, and nobody knew who they were or that they even existed. I only found out about the scheme long after I had left and gone to sea such was the secrecy. For me the sea cadets was a chance to meet other lads of my own age and experience naval discipline and procedure for the first

Dave Devey: Back row, 4th from left.

time. We did rope work and knots and learnt to drill with rifles and head the march on the local parades on festive days. I remember one time when I went down to the naval barracks at Whale Island, Portsmouth for a gunnery course in the depths of winter. It was the winter of 1957 when there was a large outbreak of Asian flu and the class of cadets from all over the country from Fleetwood in the north to Chingford in London started to succumb to the bug. Out of a class of forty, two of us were left standing on the last day, and I was one of them. However, I did not escape, as I fell ill on the train going back to Liverpool, and spent the rest of the week in bed at home. But I had finished the course and was awarded my gunnery badge which I could proudly sew on to my sleeve and for me that was a big moment.

In joining the sea cadets, it came into conflict with my obligations as a pupil at a school that hosted a combined cadet force. It was expected of everyone to dutifully join up and participate in military activities which involved having to join the army cadets as step to later joining the naval section after a period of two years. For me this presented a problem as I was primarily interested in a naval career and did not wish to be involved in army procedures as well. I was already issued with a naval uniform from the Sea Cadet Corps which required regular cleaning and maintaining and the prospects of having to upkeep and maintain an army uniform in addition did not fill me with enthusiasm. The alternative was to join the Pioneer Corps, which involved performing menial tasks mostly cleaning the vicar's motorbike and sweeping up dead leaves. Reluctantly I chose that path, along with other boys who were mostly conscientious objectors or simply didn't want to be in the army, but as a result we were looked down on by our colleagues as an inferior class of people. I lived with that stigma for the remaining years I spent at school, but looking back I feel justified in taking that decision as my only goal was to succeed as a sea cadet and advance my chances of ultimately becoming a pilot.

One of the activities for the cadets at T.S. Seahawk was to take a trip out on one of the four pilot cutters which daily plied out to Point Lynas situated some 50 miles from Liverpool off the coast of Anglesey carrying pilots out to the western station cutter where they would eventually be boarded on ships bound to the Mersey. This was a great adventure as it often involved spending the night on board and returning home the next day. The sea could also be rough, and a bout of sea sickness frequently went with the trip, but it was fascinating to watch the apprentices at work lifting and lowering the small motorboats (called punts) which took the pilots across to their ships. It would one day be my turn to learn the skills involved in such an operation which was not without its pitfalls as I will later describe. To me these lads were unsung heroes as only those present could fully appreciate the dangers involved each time they lowered a punt into a pitching sea, and frequently in the darkness of night. There were four pilot ships (known as cutters) serving the Liverpool Pilot Service which rotated duties on a weekly basis. For a week, one of the cutters would act as the Mersey Bar station, situating itself some 16 miles out to sea from the Liverpool Pier Head waterfront where the famous 'Three Graces' buildings proudly stand. The cutter assigned as the Mersey Bar station acted as the principal point for the boarding of pilots onto vessels inward to the Mersey from the north, and the disembarking of pilots outward bound from the various ports on the River Mersey, which as well as Liverpool, include Birkenhead, Tranmere Oil Jetty, Bromborough, Garston, and the entrance to the Manchester ship canal at Eastham Locks.

Point Lynas (Anglesey), Bar Station vessel and Pier Head terminal.

Main areas covered by marine pilots on the river Mersey.

Following a week at sea, the cutter that had been acting as the Mersey Bar station would return to Liverpool Landing Stage and begin a week of tender duties which involved a daily trip to the western station at Point Lynas on the Island of Anglesey, carrying a complement of pilots both for the new Bar station cutter that had replaced it, and the Lynas cutter to replace those pilots previously boarded the day before.

The pilots lived, ate and slept aboard the cutters until it was their turn to be boarded on a vessel. Each cutter was crewed by two master pilots and 15 apprentices called boat hands with a staff of two engineers, a cook and steward and two galley boys. It could carry a complement of as many as 30 pilots if circumstances necessitated though the daily complement for Lynas was fifteen pilots and ten for the Bar station. Communications in those days was extremely limited and quite often the first indication of a vessel's arrival would be a puff

Sir Thomas Brocklebank 1

Arnet Robinson 2

Edmund Garnier 3

William Clark 4

The cutters.

of smoke on the horizon followed by exchanges of signals using a morse lamp to identify the name of the vessel and to which port she was bound. Having established this information a suitably licenced pilot would be alerted and ultimately boarded on the vessel by a motor punt crewed by two apprentices. Having transferred the pilots across to the western station pilot boat the tender boat would pick up any outward pilots and return to the Bar station some 35 miles to the eastward and collect any outward pilots from the Bar boat and return to the landing stage at the Pier Head where the pilots would be landed ashore. Following a week on tender duty, the cutter would then proceed to Point Lynas and take up station there for one week when she would finally return to Liverpool to spend one week in the dock system for overhaul and repairs. This completed the four-week rotation period and following a week in dock she would sail again to take up station at the Bar. As a sea cadet you would join the tender boat at the landing stage at about eleven in the morning and sail at midday for the Bar station and then on westwards to Point Lynas returning in the late evening or early next morning to Liverpool. This experience served to convince me that my future career lay in pilotage providing of course that I could get accepted, and from then on, I set out my stall to try to make this happen.

Back at Birkenhead School I wasn't the best of pupils now I look back on it and could only wait for my sixteenth birthday when I could apply to the Pilot Service to seek an interview. The rules were very clear and invited candidates aged sixteen to apply on the understanding that if not accepted by the age of sixteen and a half they would cease to be eligible. However, if you did not succeed at the first attempt it was open to you to try again. On my birthday I duly submitted my application. I think that one of the factors in my favour was that I had been awarded "Best Cadet of the Year" that year by the sea cadet unit and had also captained the football team. I was duly granted an interview at the pilot office in Liverpool which was situated in a red brick building on the river wall at Canning Dock and now serves as part of the maritime museum. I arrived on the day all scrubbed and polished to be joined by fifteen other candidates all seeking a career as a Liverpool Pilot. We all had to sit on a long bench until it was our turn to be called into a large room with the biggest polished table I have ever seen in my life and made to stand in front of a group of elderly gentlemen all seeking to ask me questions about myself. It put me in mind of that famous painting "The Blue Boy" and "When did you last see your father?" I somehow managed to hide the fact that I was quietly knocking at the knees and was thankful that I had gone into long trousers only weeks before. I remembered what colour the funnels of the pilot boats were which was one of the questions

William Frederick Yeames:
When did you last see your father?

that probably scraped me home as I found to my delight sometime later that I had been accepted along with one other boy whose father was a pilot. I could not wait for the school year to finish and start my career as a trainee pilot, but I was already faced with a big problem and that was money. As part of the training, I needed to spend a period of time at sea as a cadet in order to learn the ways of ships and their management. To do this I needed to purchase all the items of clothing necessary for life at sea, both in European waters and in the tropics. I also had to choose my shipping company.

CHAPTER THREE: SEATIME

I didn't have much hesitation in choosing the shipping company for which I was required to spend my early years of training at sea. Alfred Holt and Company, more famously known as The Blue Funnel Line, were the most well-known line to sail out of Birkenhead and Liverpool bound for China and the far east. All their vessels were named after mythical Greek characters such as Patroclus, Hector, and Menelaus, and were easily identified by their distinctive blue funnel sited squarely amidships. The fleet consisted of some ninety-nine vessels, the story abounding at the time being that if it should exceed one hundred,

Blue Funnel Line Poster.

then the shipping company would be obliged to finance the building of a vessel for the Royal Navy. I never did find out if that story was true or not, but now I was mixing with people who abounded in tales of far-off lands with just enough credulity to convince one of their authenticity, and that was one of the stories floating round at the time. But now I was facing the real world that existed outside the sheltered cloisters of the school environment and I had to address my first problem - 'money'. I needed to be kitted out for the life at sea which included uniforms and clothing for both the warm tropical climates and the colder European weather, all of which required a substantial sum of money. With my mother as the sole breadwinner barely making ends meet, we simply didn't have that kind of cash. Through the auspices of our local Labour MP (Member of Parliament), we were put in touch with The Marine Society who were able to provide the required sum as an interest free loan, so off I went to the local naval outfitters 'Greenbergs of Park Lane' and took my first step in a life at sea, a life which ultimately concluded some forty-eight years later in 2006 with my retirement from the Liverpool Pilotage Service. Looking back at that act of financial assistance which enabled me to fulfil my dreams of becoming a pilot, it had a great effect on my future perception of life and how it is lived out by people of differing backgrounds. It served to heighten my sympathies towards those who are less well-endowed and as a result I leaned quite strongly towards left wing thinking. That was to get me labelled a communist in later life, but I was never persuaded of that view and would have accepted the tag socialist quite happily. I was and still am a practicing Christian, so I feel that the tag 'communist' was a little over the top.

I was accepted by the Blue Funnel Line as a cadet and was instructed to attend at the Midshipmen's Department situated on the fourth floor of India Buildings in Dale Street, Liverpool. I arrived there on Monday morning promptly at 0900 hours to be greeted by the avuncular figure of Captain Richards a retired deck officer within the Company whose task it was to teach a group of young men aged between sixteen and twenty the rudiments of navigation whilst waiting for their next posting to a vessel of the fleet. He was a very likeable man and somehow managed to hold the attentions of what might be described as a boisterous group of young men by his sheer ability to pass on his knowledge of the intricacies of life at sea. As a result, life at the navigation school was both orderly and enjoyable. The midshipmen resided at a hostel called "Riversdale" situated four miles to the south of India Buildings on the banks of the Mersey and each day they were bussed into the city and studied from nine till four when they were bussed back. The weekends were intended for further studies, but I suspect that the lure of nightlife in the city might have been too much for one or two of them, witnessed by their appearance at school on Monday morning. I myself was able to commute each day from my home in Tranmere taking the bus and the now famous ferry across the Mersey to the Pierhead and then walk up Dale Street to India Buildings. I spent some months at the school until Captain Richards called me in to say I had been appointed, along with three other midshipmen to the vessel Menesteus berthed at Gladstone Dock in the north end of Liverpool docks. We were to proceed with the vessel on what was designated a "coastal trip" which took in the ports of Glasgow, Antwerp, Bremen and Amsterdam. As a pilot cadet I worked alongside my fellow midshipmen and did all the duties that were allocated to them by the

The Menesteus.

chief officer who was designated our guide and mentor for the duration of the trip. No sooner were we on board ship and settled into the "half deck" which was the name given to our living quarters, than we were instructed to change into working clothes and set the task of cleaning out the bilges (sewage system) in each hatch, all of which had blocked up and could not be pumped out. The liquid content would of course be pee, of which the bulk would have been attributed to the dock workers who have spent long periods of time working in the hold without relief (no pun intended). That was my introduction to life at sea and set a pattern for the rest of my time as an apprentice both at sea and in the Pilot Service. Any job that you couldn't ask the sailors to do, get the middies out! That particular job entailed filling buckets of 'liquid' using a sooji wad and ringing it out by hand into buckets which were then hauled to the surface using a light line and subsequently dumped over the side. Needless to say the only ones who enjoyed this task were the fish that were still alive in the somewhat polluted dock water which seemed to thrive on such fare. The most junior cadet invariably got the dirtiest job and of course that was me this time. Three days and many showers later I could still smell the aroma on my person.

Very soon it was time to sail and each cadet was allocated to a post. The senior cadet was stationed on the ship's bridge, where the navigation of the vessel took place, in order to assist the second mate in recording and relaying all the various instructions which would be required in the manoeuvring operation. These would include directions to the engine room via the ship's telegraph indicating which way to turn the engine and at what speed, "dead slow, slow, half or full" (direct drive from the bridge did not exist then) and instructions to the helmsman (the person who steers the ship) as to which way to put the rudder - "port, starboard or midships" (left, right or centre). The ship's master would also be present along with the pilot who would be in charge of the navigation of the vessel whilst it remained in pilotage waters. Another cadet would be posted forward along with the chief officer who would supervise the tasks needed in the ensuing manoeuvres. These would include attaching the head tug boat to the vessel which would be required in the towing manoeuvre, the letting go of the mooring ropes, and to have ready the anchor in case it was needed. The third cadet would take station aft (rear) with the third mate also dealing with the ropes which hold the ship to the quay and the making fast (securing) of the stern (rear) tug. I was allocated to assist with the gangway which also included the rigging of a rope ladder which would be used by the pilot when he was leaving the vessel to descend to the waiting launch boat which would take him back to the shore.

With all the ropes on board and a tug attached at each end, we then proceeded through the dock system to Gladstone Lock from where the ship was lowered down to the level of the river. With the assistance of the tugs and the ship's engines, the vessel was guided out of the lock and into the River Mersey where it was swung some 180 degrees before continuing on through the main channel down to the open sea some thirteen miles away. The spring tides at Liverpool can rise and fall over ten meters twice daily and therefore the operation of an enclosed dock system is essential in the port operation. We were now at sea and bound to Glasgow, our first port of call. My duties as the most junior cadet was to scrub out the half deck each morning at seven and then change into uniform at eight along with the other cadets to attend the officers saloon where breakfast would be served by uniformed stewards in immaculate white jackets. Everything was pristine from the cutlery to the beautiful white tablecloths with a good choice of menu. Throughout my time spent on various different ships in the Blue Funnel fleet, including the subsidiary Glen Line which operated out of London, this excellent standard of catering ran right through the Company. The stewards were mostly from Liverpool and were invariably gay with that amazing sense of humour that goes with their community. One of them, Butch, once confided in me that his burning ambition was to "Hang out of a middy and later to sail with him as skipper" This translated into English would read "My greatest lifetime's wish is to have sex with a midshipman and later sail on the same ship when he has reached the rank of captain." I have to confess that I was a bit cautious when I saw him from then on, just in case he had me in mind, as that wasn't my kind of thing.

Following the brief pleasure of looking and acting like a privileged guest to dinner, it was time to strip off again and put on working gear and resume the life of a sea-bound Cinderella. I was put on day work, which involved any and every task set by the chief mate. This one went by the name of Alken, who had been given the title 'Bastard Alken' by his fellow officers and crew who had served with him on previous ships. The title did not emanate from a glance of his birth certificate, but simply from his bombastic attitude towards his fellow men, and in particular to lesser mortals who had the misfortune to be placed under his wing. I was very soon to find out why he held that title. My limited knowledge of ship-born life was soon to be exposed and worse than that, right under the nose of B. Alken. My task for that morning was to attempt to apply white paint to the salt encrusted and wet surface of the bridge wing dodger in a force 8 gale with spray whistling over the top. My mistake was to set the paint pot on the ship's wooden rail which afforded me some shelter from the ice-cold wind that was buffeting the ship. What I hadn't taken into account was that ships sometimes roll and leaving a pot of paint on the rail is not a good idea. End result: paint pot lands on pristine scrubbed wooden deck and empties its contents thereon. Who is standing watching this debacle? Yes. B……d Alken. What served to compound the misdemeanour was that the Menestheus was the newest vessel in the fleet and was on her maiden voyage from the builder's yard on the Clyde. I couldn't have committed a worse crime in the eyes of Mr. Alken. When his apoplexy had finally subsided and he had run out of expletives to describe my incompetence he directed me as to how I must attempt to reinstate his once immaculate deck to something as near to, if not better than what it had been before. I was issued with a bucket of paraffin and a bag of waste rags for the removal of the paint followed by a large holystone (a cut sandstone) which needed both hands to operate along with a bucket of water and made to rub this heavy stone over the affected decking on my hands and knees until such time as all traces of paint had been obliterated. That took most of the rest of the day with the ship heaving and rolling and me feeling decidedly ill into the bargain. Welcome to life at sea!

We completed the coastal trip and picked up our Liverpool Pilot at Holyhead whence we returned to the Mersey docking into Birkenhead where we would complete loading for the Far East at the Cathcart Street berth in Vittoria Dock. Blue Funnel used their own company pilots who were seconded from the Liverpool Pilot Service, and they preferred to use Holyhead in north Wales for the purposes of boarding and disembarking rather than use the conventional pilot station situated at Point Lynas on the Isle of Anglesey. This was intended as a guarantee of the availability of a pilot, as the vagaries of the weather in the Irish Sea sometimes prevented the station pilot boats from operating. In a strong northerly wind, the Lynas station boat would head up to the Isle Of Man and seek the shelter of Douglas Bay in order to board the ships, whilst the Bar station boat would proceed up-river to an anchorage off Woodside in Birkenhead. This was not acceptable to Blue Funnel who ran a very tight schedule and did not countenance any diversions which might result in lost time and therefore lost revenue. They even went as far as to send their pilots to the port immediately prior to Liverpool if there was any doubt as to the weather conditions at Holyhead.

On the morning of November 22nd, 1958, we sailed from Birkenhead bound for the far eastern ports of Singapore, Hong Kong and Kobe, Japan. Here I was, a sixteen-year-old, in a completely strange world with very little idea of how it all worked but very willing to do what might be asked of me. Soon the cold waters of Biscay and the north Atlantic would be replaced with the warmer climes of the Mediterranean although it was still cold with a need to keep well wrapped up from the winter weather. I was now earning the princely sum of £10 per month but I was well happy as my board and lodge was free and a round tin of 50 Players cigarettes cost only 2 shillings and six pence (about 25p in today's money) which was deducted from my pay account kept by the chief steward. In those days most people smoked as it was not considered harmful, and the movie stars were frequently seen puffing away setting the example to everyone else. Life was pleasant at sea without all the hassle that went with entering or leaving port, and we soon settled down to enjoying the Mediterranean weather and the added luxury of regular mealtimes, always mindful that when Butch was the serving steward, that I was not an invitation to him to succeed in his ambitions with me, though I should have realised at the time that as a pilot cadet he could not fulfil his intentions as I would finish up as a pilot and not a ship's master. This idyllic situation was not to last however, as news came through the grapevine that we were diverting course to Malta due to engine problems so all preparations had to be made ready for berthing. We arrived that afternoon at grand Harbour Valetta and proceeded past the numerous warships both British and American to moor stern first to the quay. With evening approaching we were called into Mr. Alken's presence on the bridge who informed us that we would all be required to simultaneously lower all flags that were currently flying right on the stoke of sunset. These would include the small company house flag flown at the jack staff forward, the Maltese courtesy ensign, the large Company house flag flown from the mainmast on a ricker and the red ensign at the stern. We were going to show the navy that we weren't slouches and could match their drill procedures with the same precision. Mr. Alken stood next to the ship's chronometer and at precisely sunset that day he would blow a loud blast on his pea whistle to signal the procedure to commence. Sunset duly arrived, the shrill piercing note of the referee's whistle sounded, and the four flags were lowered with military precision. The only problem was that the military were not quite as precise. Some many minutes later a lone AB sauntered up to the quarterdeck of the largest British warship and nonchalantly pulled down the ensign followed by an American sailor even more nonchalantly strolling aft whilst pulling on a lucky strike from the corner of his mouth before hauling down the Stars and Stripes. Life was very different out there as I was very soon to find out. We were given shore leave that evening and off we all went "sight-seeing". Little did I in my innocence realise what sight-seeing meant. I was dragged down the red-light district of Valetta to an infamous area known locally as "the Gut". This consisted of brothel after brothel with ladies plying their trade in fierce competition for customers. Matters were made worse by my colleagues pointing at me and shouting "Cherry boy!" to the ladies of the night. This evoked a similar reaction as moths do to a flame with women who were old enough to be my mother yanking at my jacket and shouting "Come in here for f...ks sake!" And they meant it literally. I somehow managed to fend them off and escape back to the ship without losing my virginity much to the amusement of my fellow shipmates.

We sailed the next morning and dutifully dipped our ensign to the many warships of different nationalities which were visiting Malta at the time with some reciprocating and others not. We saw it as a courtesy we should not ignore irrespective of the response and once we had dropped the pilot, we were on our way with the engines now repaired and the telegraphs at "full ahead" and bound for Port Said where we would begin our journey through the Suez canal and into the Red Sea. It was Sunday when we arrived at Port Said where we loaded 40 tons of onions before entering the Canal itself. No sooner had we started our passage than we were joined by a number of bumboats – small boats with traders selling all manner of goods. The Egyptians were euphoric following their 'victory' in the recent Suez War and were selling commemorative postage stamps depicting heroic Egyptian soldiers parachuting out of the sky and descending onto surrendering British soldiers. We were instructed to keep a low profile and not to get involved in any politically sensitive issues which might jeopardise our rite of passage. Amongst the many traders were such characters as 'Rifle-eye' and the 'Gully Gully Man'. The latter would arrive with 3 small cups under one of which would be a ball. He would challenge anyone to guess which cup the ball was under after quickly shuffling them round to the magic words "gully gully". I never guessed right in all the attempts I made to outwit him, and I didn't see anyone else beat him either. One of the traders asked me if I would like to buy "humbugs" and, thinking in my naivety "what is an Egyptian doing selling sweets?" when he pulled out from under his caftan some ladies handbags. "These foreigners do speak strangely", I thought! We proceeded through the Canal in convoy at a steady 8 knots till we reached the Bitter Lakes where we anchored to let the northbound convoy through. Then it was on our way through the last leg of the journey to Port Suez where we exited the Canal and entered the Red Sea. The temperature quickly rose as we steamed south, and the instruction went out to change from blue uniforms to the cooler dress of white shirts and shorts. For me, this meant a change to khaki shorts and shirt as my time was spent cleaning, painting, and scrubbing, apart from those brief interludes of attendance in the dining saloon when I could dress up in my nice white uniform and pretend to be a human being instead of some sort of serf. The warmer weather heralded the construction of the canvas swimming pool which was erected on the well deck forward of the bridge by the chippy. It was our task to assist him in fixing the metal poles into place and then stretching the canvas over them whence the pool could be filled with sea water. It was always a pleasure to me when the day's work was over to be able to go for a swim in the pool, especially when the ship was gently rolling, as the motion of the ship would create waves in the pool just like the open sea. We could now settle down to a few days of sunshine and uninterrupted sailing until we reached Aden, where we briefly called in to take on fuel (bunkers) after which we set course east across the Indian Ocean bound for Singapore. It is a pleasant part of the voyage crossing the Indian Ocean with flying fish appearing to race the ship and sometimes landing on deck as a result of over exuberance, but with all hands totally engaged in their daily duties there was no one available to rescue them and send them back from where they came. It bothered me to see these creatures suffering without any help but again it was one of the many things I had to come to accept as normal practice in the life at sea. Everybody had a job to do and unless it was an emergency which this was clearly not you stuck to the task. Somebody would ultimately have the job sometime in the early evening of clearing the scuppers of the unfortunate fish and throw them overboard before they blocked the drainage of sea water from the main deck. During this seven-day sea passage it was also a time to hone one's skills at steering the vessel, and early attempts would result in what's known as "Writing your initials in the sea". It only became apparent when your trick of two hours was over, and the officer of the watch would make you look aft to see the wake from the propeller. With good steering it should be a straight line; with a beginner it was anything but. I also enjoyed the evenings after sunset when it was possible to practice on the morse lamp and signal to passing vessels. It helped to break the monotony of watch-keeping during a prolonged period at sea with no sight of land. A colleague once told me an amusing incident he had when morsing another ship. He sent "What ship?" which is the customary opening gambit when communicating in the morse code to which the

SS Reina Del Mar.

other vessel replied "Flagship Reina Del Mar" to which he sent back "What Company?" The responding lamp went quickly dead. You could almost hear the other ship's officer retorting "Bloody cheek!" All these learning skills would come into play some many years later in the run up to achieving the ultimate goal of a pilot's licence. The experience I gained as a cadet with Blue Funnel proved to be an ideal introduction to the kind of life I would be expected to follow as a boat hand in the Liverpool Pilot service some years later. The daily tasks we were allotted whilst at sea were mostly concerned with maintaining the upkeep and appearance of the vessel which included painting the lifeboats, chipping, scraping and red-leading the rails, polishing the brass work on the bridge, and scrubbing the decks clean after the disruption of each harbour visit. When in harbour, it was cleaning out the hatches ready for loading cargo and to keep watches safeguarding the cargo, and in particular the large amount of mail that we carried.

Soon the bliss of life at sea was to end and the preparations for the arrival at the Singapore pilot station had to be made. I was assigned to assist in the rigging of the pilot ladder on the leeward side of the ship (the side sheltered from the wind). A rope ladder of some 30 feet in length was secured to the rail and thrown over the side along with 2 manropes one on each side for the pilot to use when hauling himself up the ship's side. A lifebelt was made ready and a heaving line for the pilot's bag. The gangway was then rigged and swung out ready to be lowered to a point where it met the rope ladder, and the pilot was able to transfer onto it before the final climb to the main deck. As the pilot launch arrived alongside it was my duty to throw down the heaving line to the boat where the AB (able seaman) then attached the bag, and I then hauled it on board. Once safely on board and in possession of his bag I escorted the pilot through the accommodation area and up the various stairways to the navigating bridge where he met the captain to discuss the forthcoming passage to the berth in Singapore Harbour. Everyone would then take up their allotted stations ready for docking. Sometimes the passage would take many hours and mealtimes had to be staggered or in some cases abandoned altogether. We were now on the Malay coast and life would be punctuated by frequent "standbys" entering or leaving ports. To me as a sixteen-year-old, the whole thing was fascinating and extremely exciting visiting these ports for the first time and witnessing the many different cultures that exist on the far side of the world. Singapore proved to be very beautiful and a visit to Raffles Square was a must, but I sensed that everyone seemed to be saving themselves for the big one i.e. Hong Kong which was the next but one port and the second home for the Blue Funnel Line after its home port of Liverpool. It was Christmas Day in Singapore, and we were invited aboard a Ben Line vessel where we were royally entertained and returned to our own ship Menestheus for a slap-up Christmas dinner care of the catering staff. I had been told that it was the custom for the youngest officer in the saloon to make a speech to the other officers and I duly rehearsed my lines until I had them off perfect. Sadly, someone forgot to ask me to speak, and I left the saloon very disappointed as I had saved up a few swipes at our illustrious Chief Officer Mr. Alken. Perhaps he knew they were coming and blocked my big chance. I'll never know.

Our next port was Bangkok where we anchored off and discharged into lighters. I was struck with the beauty of the ladies selling their wares from the sampans tied up alongside and all wearing these round straw hats. We traded bars of soap with them in exchange for fresh mangoes and paw paws. I passed my 17th birthday here and bought a bottle of Bangkok whisky with the intention of taking it home on my return to the UK. Little did I realise that it was just firewater as we were soon to discover when celebrating my birthday on December 28[th.] The other cadets had persuaded me of the stupidity of keeping this bottle of whisky to take home as we would each be allowed a docking bottle of Scotch whisky or gin prior to docking in Liverpool. One of the cadets had been given some cans of Guinness which had been found abandoned in the hold from a damaged case. All the ingredients were there for a party. Firstly, it was somebody's birthday. Secondly, a bottle of local whisky and third some warm cans of Guinness, plus four guys with the evening free. What do you think happened next? Yes, you guessed it! A large bowl, pour in the Guinness, top it up with Bangkok whisky with a stamp on the label guaranteeing that it had been made that day, and you have the perfect punch. Or so we all thought at the time. That night I turned in to my bunk which was on the bottom, and my colleague Pat climbed into his bunk above mine. At about 0200 I was awakened by a warm feeling of something sticky trickling through my hair and down my neck and the sound of moaning coming from the top bunk. It was Pat, who had decided that he needed to part company with this unpleasant cocktail of Guinness and whisky. It was the one and only time that we drank alcohol whilst on board. I think we had all learnt our lesson following king size hangovers the next day.

Soon we were ready to sail again and this time it was to Hong Kong. I could sense an air of apprehension in the crew as though they had all been waiting for this moment and I was not disappointed. Hong Kong was known as the gem of the orient and it rightly proved to be the case. No sooner had we arrived than the merchants were thronging around selling their various wares. Your foot was placed on a piece of leather and the outline drawn in chalk by one trader selling shoes whilst another had a tape measure sizing you up for a tailor-made suit. All this with the patter of "No need pay this time. I catch you next time if you no have money". They were true as their word and would only take what you could afford at that time and put you on their account. Everything was incredibly cheap by UK standards, and we were able to trade cigarettes for Hong Kong dollars. The rate of exchange at that time was $16HK to £1UK and even we cadets could afford the prices. We were not allowed any alcohol whilst on board, but a trip ashore offered the chance to catch a beer in one of the many bars. Our favourite haunt was Henrys Café in Kowloon after visiting the local barber's salon for a haircut. A haircut in Hong Kong was the nearest you could experience to a sex act but only paying $1. On entering the salon, you would be greeted by a very beautiful girl who would usher you to a leather couch where you would be asked to lie down with your head cradled in a basin with the lady's hands underneath your head for support. Warm soapy water would then be poured over the scalp, while massaging fingers were applied the follicles. Please check the dictionary for the word "Follicles" before you read on. By this time, you would experience a pleasant drowsiness created by the soft tones of the lady's voice asking you if the water was warm enough. This lasted for an all too brief a time, when the water was replaced by a warm towel and the massaging continued until the hair was dry enough to escort you, whilst still in dreamland to the comfort of a leather chair and the offer of a lucky strike cigarette, carefully lit by an electric sparked lighter. This was heaven after five weeks at sea in all male company. A choice of glossy magazines was proffered, which helped to further enhance the feeling of being in heaven at last, but all too soon it was time to come down to earth with a show of the mirror and a handshake with a tip for a job well done. I fell in love with one of the waitresses in Henry's Café and showered her with generous tips in the hope of winning her affections, but sadly there was no response to my overtures and when it came time to sail for Japan, I was still without a girlfriend to write to. Due to the ongoing confrontation between the Chinese Nationalist Government and the Government of Taiwan, we were obliged to circumnavigate the island and travel up its east side, as the two warring factions were busy firing shells at each other, and we weren't prepared to take the chance of one falling short of its target. For me, one of the most pleasant times of the day at sea was in the evening following dinner. I would wander down to the main deck just aft of the accommodation next to number 5 hatch. There I would meet up with the bosun Mike (Mick) Finlay who always had a good yarn to tell. He was a Canadian by birth and had not lost his accent in his fifty odd years of life at sea. He was fiercely anti-Japanese and told me that he would not go ashore on arrival in Japan, as he had been held as a prisoner of war by the Japanese following the fall of Singapore during the second world war. He was an amiable man and had a wonderful sense of humour, sometimes bordering on the wicked. I remember one evening we were chatting away when one of the deck boys, a scouser called Joe, happened to be passing on the opposite side to us and walking aft towards the sailor's accommodation. He was a tall and muscular lad of about sixteen and the youngest of the deck crew. Mick said to me in a loud voice (that he knew Joe could hear) "Hey Mid (midshipman). Look at Joey here. There is a fine example of a strong… young…healthy…strapping (at which point Joe looks across with a big smile on his face lapping up the plaudits from his boss) useless C—T!", at which point the beaming smile turned into a sheepish grin and Joe continued on his way aft.

Kobe was to be our last port of discharge and one could not help but be impressed by the industrious nature of the Japanese people. Everybody was busy going somewhere or doing something with no time to stop to chat. But Kobe did not have the charm and sheer friendliness of Hong Kong, and whilst very beautiful and immaculately clean, it was somewhat cold to me. It was also cold weather-wise, and we were all back in blues and wrapped up against the bitter winds. I did go ashore on a shopping trip and saw a most beautiful bone china tea set and decided to buy it for my mother along with a bright red lacquered music box in which a dancing lady popped up to the sound of Japanese music when the lid was opened. The shops were full of the most exquisite children's toys which were far more beautiful and mechanically advanced than anything on sale in post-war Britain. On our departure from Kobe we were serenaded by a brass band belonging to the Japanese Customs and Excise who played "Sayonara, Japanese goodbye" to the tearful sailors with the ladies of the night gaily waving items of underwear as a token of their undying love.

We are now homeward bound at last and back to Hong Kong to start loading for Liverpool. We returned home via Singapore and then on to Port Swettenham in Malaysia aptly named for its humid climate where we loaded bales of rubber and palm oil into heated deep tanks. My job was to take the ullage of the deep tanks and record the daily temperatures from three thermometers strung at intervals from a chain which reached all the way to the bottom of the tank. Each evening after dinner I would do my rounds and note down the temperatures of each tank. Afterwards, my hands would be covered in palm oil before I could wipe them clean with some waste cloths and return the chain to the depths of the bucket I was keeping them in. As a result, I ended up as the person with the most beautiful hands of anyone on board. They were as good as any ladies' hands I might have come into contact with including the hairdresser in the Hong Kong salon.

After Port Swettenham we sailed for Penang, where we loaded more rubber and tin ingots in preparation for the return journey to Liverpool. Most of our work whilst we were in port was spent down in the hatches keeping a cargo watch. The humidity level was very high and after a few hours your shirt would be saturated with sweat and required a change of clothes, sometimes two or three times in a day. We had to do our own washing, so the early evening was spent dhobying our clothes ready for the next spell of duty down the hold. But soon it was time to sail, and we were once more heading west to the Port of Colombo on the island of Ceylon (now called Sri Lanka) where we loaded large wooden boxes of tea. On again westwards and into the Gulf Of Aden to a port on the east coast of Africa named Djibouti. There the temperature soared to 120 Fahrenheit with the steel hatch covers too hot to be able to touch and quite capable of frying an egg on if one was feeling hungry. The cargo to be loaded was coffee in large sacks which were heavy and needed a strong person to carry just one of them. The African workers were up to the task as each one was tall and athletically built. They wore only a cloth around their waste for protection from the sun's burning rays. As each sack was loaded onto the back of the carrier the rest of the gang would chant a song which would spur the man on to reach the point where he could drop the sack into the desired position. It was back-breaking work and done in temperatures that most other workers would have flatly refused to participate, but these remarkable men kept going until every bag had been stowed and we were ready to sail again.

We now joined the north bound convoy for the passage through the Suez Canal and thoughts were beginning to turn towards home and the countdown to our arrival once more at Liverpool. The crew were developing what is known as "The Channels" in anticipation of that moment when families and friends will once more greet each other after a parting of some 4 months. There was an expression amongst the Blue Funnel crews which said, "Four to the Rock and three to the dock", which briefly sums up the average number of steaming days between leaving the Suez Canal and arriving at Liverpool. The weather in the Mediterranean had been favourable with a strong easterly wind pushing us up to seventeen and a half knots, but that soon changed following our exchange of signals with the Gibraltar lookout station. Turning into the Atlantic and heading up past the Bay of Biscay the weather now turned sour, and the ship rolled all the way up to the Saint Georges Channel and towards Holyhead where we were to pick up the Liverpool Pilot. The crew had opened a book where everyone could make a bet on the time of arrival at the pilot station with the exact moment that the pilot would set his foot on the bottom rung of the pilot ladder. The person with the nearest time to that moment would sweep the prize. We arrived at the pilot station at 1600 hours on Friday 20th November 1959 and proceeded towards Liverpool where we docked into Gladstone Lock some three months and three weeks after leaving our berth in Birkenhead.

I was to do another two voyages before the time came for me to join the Liverpool Pilot Service as trainee pilot. One of them was with a subsidiary company of Blue Funnel called Glen Line, which was based in London and whose funnels were red and not blue. The crew were all Chinese including the sailors working on deck. I joined the ship in Saint Katherines Dock along with 3 other cadets, two of whom were Scotsmen, and one was an old Etonian called Nigel who had been sent there by management to just do the one voyage in order to learn the ropes of ship-born life. As you can imagine, Nigel was very different to the rest of us "rough and toughy" northerners but did his best to integrate and learn the ways of the sea in the limited time he had. The only source of friction came when we arrived in port, and he would be ushered off ashore with the visiting ship's agent to be cosseted by management before returning to the ship prior to sailing. In the meantime, the rest of us would be sweating down the hatches doing cargo watch or any other duties that were thrust upon us. But overall life on board was pleasant with the ship's master Captain Letty forever unpredictable in his behaviour, particularly when he had had a couple of snifters. On one occasion in the Mediterranean, he threw a lifebelt overboard and shouted to the watch-keeping officer "Man overboard!"

The officer was taken totally by surprise and presumed someone had gone over the side and pressed the alarm bells alerting all the crew to lifeboat stations. The ship was turned full round in the designated textbook procedure and a reverse course was steered to look for the unfortunate person. The ship was slowed down and two lifeboats were launched. A search went on until sunset when all hopes of any rescue were abandoned. It was only after a head count of all crew members showed that everyone was present that the realisation dawned that no one was actually missing. The only things lost were the lifebelt and a half day steaming time which would not have gone down too well with management when they eventually heard the story. I wonder whether Nigel kept it to himself as a dutiful member of crew, or did his management upbringing come to the surface when it came to affairs of economy? The upshot of it all was that the crew's response to the emergency was highly commendable given the circumstances, and the exercise proved a very useful drill in the event of a real "man overboard" situation. Captain Letty's unpredictable behaviour came to the fore again sometime later in the voyage, but this time involving myself. We had just picked up the Hong Kong pilot, and on his arrival on the bridge Captain Letty said to me in a loud voice "You're a Liverpool Pilot! You can take us in today!" I was naturally taken aback as a sixteen-year-old cadet and promptly froze on the spot to be put out of my embarrassment by the real pilot, who ignored what had just happened and carried on as normal. However, I resolved there and then that should he ever pull that trick again, I would be ready for him and respond differently. My turn was to come sooner than I expected. This time we were on passage up the creeks to Reyjang in Sarawak with the pilot already giving instructions to the helmsman on what course to steer. I was on bridge standby recording the times of the engine movements when captain Letty said to the pilot "I've got my own pilot on board today and he is going to take us in." He ushered me to the front of the bridge and said, "Off you go pilot!" The pilot himself was a little bemused but decided to join in the game. We were steaming at slow speed and were following the bends in the channel so it was relatively straight-forward, and I knew that the pilot would correct me if he was not happy with what I was doing. I in turn decided to be cheeky too and nonchalantly leaned against the forward bridge windows whilst calling out the next course to steer. Unfortunately for me, this behaviour caught the attention of Mr. Marshal, the Chief Mate, who was standing on the forecastle head. He was incensed that a cadet should be behaving in such a slovenly manner and telephoned up to the bridge. I could hear him over the loud phone speaking in an irate voice "What is that middy doing leaning on the bridge windows? Captain Letty snatched the phone from the second mate's hands and screamed back to the mate "Because he's the f...king PILOT!" The mate's jaw dropped in disbelief and, as a consequence, so did the phone from his hand. But normal order was to re-establish itself as we neared the berthing area, and the pilot once more took the control. I think he was as amused as I was at what took place, though I've no idea what he might have said to the harbour authorities on his return to base. But these adventures were soon to end, and in March 1960 I was called to join the Liverpool Pilot Service as a boat hand. The training that I had received whilst a cadet with Blue Funnel was to stand me in good stead for the next period of my life, which was to last for a further 6 years. I was issued with a standard Mersey Docks And Harbour Board uniform complete with cap and badge, and detailed to join pilot boat number 1 which was tied up in Egerton Dock (Birkenhead).

CHAPTER FOUR:
LIFE AS A BOATHAND

I joined Number 1 pilot boat Sir Thomas Brocklebank on a grey March morning and introduced myself to my fellow apprentices, one of whom was particularly delighted to see me. Everyone had a nick name and his was Boo Boo. The reason that Boo Boo was

Sir Thomas Brocklebank.

so happy to see me was because he would now be promoted to the position of 'chart room lad' and he would no longer be called 'junior lad'; that title would go to me. He would no longer have to scrub out the apprentice's accommodation on a daily basis, nor wash up the dirty dishes after serving them their meals. Instead, he would look after the two pilot masters who were in charge of the whole running operation of the pilot boat. Each evening after dinner, he would leave the apprentices accommodation, which was situated right aft, and walk forward to the two cabins which were housed just below the bridge. Each cabin contained a bunk, a settee, and a locker with a communal toilet, and served as home for the two pilot masters for the duration of their time spent on station. Boo Boo's job now was to keep this area clean, and mine was to look after the apprentices and to clean the cabins of the two senior lads. If I had thought that life as a cadet at sea was hard going, then I was about to find out what hard going really meant. As junior lad, my day started at 0700 hours when I would scrub out the mess room, which was home to twelve apprentices ranging in age from 18 to 24. The apprentices worked a watch system of 4 hours on duty and 4 hours off duty on a 24-hour basis for the three weeks at sea, which was interrupted each evening with a 2 hour 'dog watch' between the hours of 6 and 8 p.m. After finishing scrubbing out, I then had to get everything ready for breakfast. I had a small galley adjacent to the main mess room with a sink and a hot press for warming the plates. Breakfast would consist of porridge, followed by bacon and eggs, which needed to be collected from the ship's galley, a journey involving a flight of stairs and a trip along an alleyway. By the time the tray of eggs arrived at the mess room the fried eggs were like rocks and the bacon not much better. I later found out that they were the leftovers from the pilots' breakfasts, which had previously been on offer in their saloon. When all the apprentices were seated at table the senior lad would call "Pass in!" and that was the signal for me to produce the pan of porridge from the hot press along with the requisite number of bowls. If the bowls were not considered warm enough this could result in what was known as "a work up" for the junior lad, which meant extra duties after work time. I witnessed one senior lad pick up the first bowl then drop it on the floor where it smashed into pieces saying, "This bowl is not warm enough!" and proceeded to break the rest until the unfortunate junior lad intervened and rescued what was left. It was his job to find the replacements before the next breakfast time, which was not an easy task. The main course was bacon and eggs which came on a white enamel tray. This was then put into the hot press until it was time to serve. The senior lad served himself first, then passed the flat to the second senior lad and then it was passed down the table in order of seniority. The last one to get fed was the chart room lad, and by that time there was not much left. The eggs by now were like leather and not particularly palatable. Even a large dollop of tomato sauce could not improve the taste. Butter was only for the two senior lads, with the rest of the crew on margarine. When breakfast was over it was time to clear away the dishes and wash them up in the sink. A tin can with holes punctured in it, tied round the tap and filled with bits of Howard Baker soap, served as the cleaning agent - the same Howard Baker soap used to scrub the brown linoleum floor of the mess room. Washing up liquid as we know it hadn't been invented then, or at least if it had, it was still not available to the Pilot Service. In between mealtimes my job was to join the other boat hands up on deck and assist with the various cleaning jobs that they were performing. It served as a welcome break from being "down aft" as the only source of natural light there were a few small portholes and in heavy weather it could be uncomfortable below decks. Following the evening meal, my final job was to clean the two senior boat hands' cabins and make up their bunks. There was a special way of making up the bedding which was called a wad in the local jargon, and it needed a demonstration from Boo Boo to show me how it was done. My duties finished at 2000 hours and my daily routine would last until the next apprentice joined the job and I was promoted to chart room lad. The average period of time spent in any one stage before promotion to the next was about six months. However, it was dead men's shoes, and it could be considerably longer if there we no retirements at the top end. As a junior lad, you just kept going despite the obstacles thrown in your path, and you lived for the day when the next new recruit turned up and took over your duties. It was very much a case of learning the ropes, and fast, otherwise you didn't survive as any mistakes could lead to a work up, and too many work ups would lead to over-tiredness with a knock on effect. The attitude of the senior boat hand towards you could have a big impact on whether you would survive or not, so it was always good policy to keep him sweet. You quickly learnt to identify who might be a threat to your survival and how to treat that person until you became accepted as a fellow boat hand. It soon became apparent to me that there existed an ongoing feud between Boo Boo and another more senior apprentice whose nickname was Bear. Bear was aptly named as his real name was Ted and he was big and muscular with a large mop of curly black hair and was someone that you would not want to meet on a dark night. Despite his powerful frame he was a gentle person, but could be easily aroused if goaded, and Boo Boo who was short and nearly as wide as he was tall was the perfect foil. My first experience of this feud was soon after I had joined the boat and we were heading up towards Douglas on the Isle Of Man. The reason for this annual journey was to show a selected group of licenced pilots the different parts of the Liverpool Pilotage Area. This area encompassed the east coast of the Isle Of Man and ran from the Point Of Aire in the north of the island across to Saint Bees Head in Cumberland, and from The Chickens Rock in the south across to Middle Mouse Island off the coast of Anglesey. This annual event was known to the pilots as a "survey of the district" and chose to serve as a

Survey of the District.

little relaxation away from the daily task of guiding ships in and out of the Port of Liverpool. However, what was the pilots' gain was the apprentices' loss as these surveys were conducted when the pilot boat should have been in its off duty resting mode in dock, resulting in a loss of two days leave of duty for them. The weather on this occasion was bad with a north-westerly wind blowing at force 6-7 on the Beaufort scale with sheet rain, and us heading straight into it barely making headway. True to form, the watch on deck were given the task of painting the after-accommodation housing which served as home to the boat hands. For the benefit of the readers, I may refer to apprentices as boat hands and boat hands as apprentices. They are both the same thing. Bear was off duty and on his watch below and was in the communal bathroom getting ready for bed, with his nemesis Boo Boo outside on deck attempting to adhere gloss white paint to the wet bulkhead through the blinding rain, with the aid of a roller attached to a makeshift pole. He called out to Bear, who could not resist the urge to poke his head out of the port hole to see what was going on. Unfortunately for Bear, Boo Boo was on the upstroke of the roller just at that moment, which resulted in Bear's complexion going from bright red to snow white, with just two brown eyes visible. Boo Boo well knew the consequences should Bear ever catch up with him, and smartly disappeared to a safe haven down in the steering flat until Bear gave up the chase and retired off to bed. Meanwhile, we ploughed on against the wind and waves, and finally arrived in the shelter of Douglas Harbour on the southeast side of the island. It was pitch dark when we tied up on the outer breakwater and the boat hands were given leave to go ashore, all except me who, as junior lad, had to stay on board and keep a gangway watch in addition to tending the mooring ropes, as the harbour was tidal. It was around about eleven thirty that night and most people were back on board, when I spotted a furtive figure proceeding at a gallop towards me with what appeared to be a lantern in his hand. As he passed me before disappearing below decks, (as he had become quite adept at disappearing when the going got hot) Boo Boo thrust the object into my hand. It was a cocky watchman's oil lamp which was used to mark road works at night and was still lit. Hard on his heels was an officer of the law who promptly seized me by the arm crying "Gotcha, ya thieving little bugger!" He had apprehended the villain red handed, or so he thought. Any protest was useless, and he frog marched me back to the spot where the lamp had originally stood some twenty minutes' walk away and made me replace it on the spot from where it had gone missing. I was now starting to get worried as the Isle Of Man penal system advocated birching as the punishment for vandalism and I would be seen as a vandal by the general public. However, the officer in question decided to take a lenient view of the incident and lectured me as to my future behaviour. I was duly penitent promising never to repeat such a wicked act and breathed a sigh of relief when I was able to return to the boat with my rear end still intact. We left Douglas next morning and headed up to Saint Bees Head in Cumbria where we then turned south and proceeded to Morecambe Bay, finally finishing in Morecambe where we spent the night before returning back to Liverpool. A comedian once said that Morecambe was a place where they didn't bury their dead but stood them up in bus shelters. Well, on a winter's night in March with a gale blowing and lashing rain, I don't think he was too far wrong.

I now fell into the routine of junior lad. The daily scrubbing out of the mess room, washing the dishes and waiting on the other apprentices at mealtimes. When not doing that, I worked on deck helping the others in their various cleaning tasks. Up until now I had been excluded from the other duties of the

Edmund Gardner punt (yellow).

boat hands which was to man the motorboats called punts that carried the pilots to and from their ships. This task involves a great deal of skill in the lowering and recovery of these punts, especially in the extreme weather conditions which prevail in the Irish Sea, and the process of learning the various roles that were involved in the procedure was usually done in relatively calm weather. However, situations do arise when normal practice is abandoned. We were anchored at the Bar station and because they were short-handed, I was called to assist in the lifting up of a punt that had been left tied alongside. The weather had worsened, and the pilot boat was still anchored, which created a situation whereby a swell (waves created by the wind) was running down both sides of the pilot boat. The punt needed to be lifted as it was taking on water. As there was nobody else available, I was told to jump into the bow (front) and make ready the lifting block. The lifting block was made of metal and housed a pulley wheel with a thick wire running through it, making the whole thing quite heavy to handle, and once engaged with the lifting hook, needed to be avoided at all costs. On this occasion the coxswain jumped into the stern (back) and received his block from a third apprentice who then operated the lifting winch motor once both blocks were engaged into their hooks. The punt was pitching heavily up and down, and as I engaged my block, I slipped forward on the wet deck boards. The weight came on to the metal block, which sprang back and caught me above the right eye. I was thrown backwards into the boat, and the next thing I remember was being tended to whilst lying on my back in the boarding embayment.

I had a rather large gash on my forehead which obviously needed stitching, and that would require a trip to hospital in Liverpool some 16 miles away. I heard the pilot master enquire down from the bridge "What's the matter with the lad?", and when told his reply was "Get him up to town!" I would have to wait until the tender boat which transported us returned from the western station at Point Lynas before I could be taken ashore. I was duly stitched up that night at the Southern Hospital and returned back to duty the next day. There was no time for rest and recovery as they were already short-handed, and my absence made the situation even worse. The happiest man on board was Boo Boo who thought I had swallowed the anchor and was not expecting me to return. His short-lived promotion to chart room lad was once more restored. Whilst no one made comment, I think my early return was met with muted approval, and together with a change of footwear to the non-slip variety, I was able to pick up the job of bow lad without any further mishaps. The bow lad's job was to get the punt ready for launching. This would involve ascending a steel ladder and climbing into the punt which was housed in the davits (a crane on the side of the ship). The drainage plug needed to be screwed into place, and the diesel engine cranked over and running, with the tiller slotted into its housing ready for the arrival of the coxswain who was in charge of the boat. If any of these tasks were not done correctly or in sufficient time, then that could incur a" work up" from the coxswain which meant extra work in the time that you should be resting after finishing duties - not forgetting that the junior lad had already done a 13-hour day! The normal working practice when launching the punt into the water began with the pilot master first making a lee (blocking the wind) with the pilot boat, thus allowing the punt to be dropped into the water on the sheltered side away from the open sea. Once the pilot boat was in position, the order would then be given to lower the punt from its stowed position in the davits. On it landing in the water, the coxswain in the stern of the punt would then pull a handle which released both blocks from their hooks. The lifting hooks are weighted so as to spring back into place on the release of the blocks and are then ready for the lifting up process. The bow rope is then released, and the punt is held alongside by the coxswain until the arrival of the pilot, whose bag is handed to the bow lad for safekeeping. Once the pilot is aboard, the bow rope is thrown to the waiting boat hand who is standing in the embayment. Again a "work up" could be incurred if the bow rope fails to reach the embayment, and believe me, they are quite heavy, especially when wet and need a really good throw to make it land safely. Once the punt is under way, the bow lad's job is to operate the hood (boat cover) which helps to protect the seas from coming over the bow and getting the pilot wet in the transfer journey to the approaching ship. On arrival alongside the ship to be boarded, the bow lad would secure the pilot's bag to the heaving line thrown down from the ship where it would be hauled up the ship's side and onto the deck. The duty officer on the ship would then take the pilot's bag and escort him to the bridge, a job that I once had myself when serving as a cadet with The Blue Funnel Line. Once the pilot had stepped onto the rope ladder, the coxswain would pull away from the ship's side and drop back to a position where he would best be able to recover him in the event of him falling into the water. Once he was safely on board, the punt would return to the pilot boat and prepare for being lifted up. The bow rope would be thrown to the bow lad who would secure it to the thaft and in heavy weather a second line called a rolling tackle (pronounced "taycal") would be passed out to him to stop the punt pitching forward in the swell (the waves created by the wind). The bow lad would take a few turns round the thaft with this tackle and then stand on the trailing end whilst receiving his hoisting block. These blocks are quite heavy and need to be treated with respect as I earlier found out to my detriment. On the command "Dig in!" from the coxswain, the bow lad would then engage the eye of the block with the lifting hook and quickly clear out of the way. Once engaged, the bow lad shouted "In forrard!" The coxswain would then engage his block and shout "In aft!" and the third apprentice would acknowledge by shouting "Fore and aft!" and start the lifting motor until the punt was once more stowed in the davits. The bow lad would then unship the plugs and allow the punt to drain of any sea water. This procedure could be followed as many as 30-40 times in any 12 hours, both in daylight and in the dark. Once the punt was safely stowed in the davits, a safety wire was clipped into place to prevent it being launched accidentally. When the punt was about to be launched, the bow lad would release this clip prior to shipping (screwing into place) the drain plugs. Both these tasks merited the dreaded "work up" should the bow lad in his haste forget to do either of them. As I have said before, survival depended on learning the ropes fast, as the system of correction could lead to less time for rest and subsequently tiredness, which would lead to more mistakes and ultimately to the boat hand's enforced resignation. The system of work ups was starting to fade out when I joined the Service in 1960, though it still continued for a number of years more. During the hours of darkness everything became more difficult when working the punts. The bow lad's job was to shine a torch alternately at the approaching ship and back to the pilot boat to indicate the position of the punt. If the torch failed for any reason, a green flare had to be ignited, and in the event of an engine failure a red flare had to be shown. The coxswain's job became doubly difficult as he needed to both keep the pilot dry, yet judge the speed of the approaching ship so as to catch it before it went past and left him having to chase it. In bad weather at night, going too fast could mean incurring the wrath of a wet pilot, with seas coming over the top of the hood, and going too slow meant missing the ship, which could result in an even wetter pilot when chasing after it. The coxswain was also responsible for the safety of all on board and a high degree of skill was required when turning the punt though 180 degrees before making the return journey back to the pilot boat. On the return journey back to the pilot boat, the bow lad would drop the hood and the punt would run before the wind and sea.

My pay as a first-year boat hand amounted to ten pounds, four shillings, and four pence in the old currency per month, which represented a cut in pay from the fourteen pounds I was paid as a second-year cadet with the Blue Funnel Line. In addition, the hours of work were considerably higher as a boat hand as I started the day at 0700 hours and finished at 2000 hours, providing I had not incurred any work ups. This daily routine was repeated seven days a week for the three weeks spent at sea, making a working week of 91 hours, with no guarantee of survival except the distant hope that you might one day join the ranks of the licenced pilots. This hope of success also depended on the result of an annual examination of proficiency which consisted of an oral examination conducted at the pilot office by the Harbour Authority with a senior pilot present. The candidate was made to stand facing a committee comprising of the Harbourmaster, the Marine Surveyor, the Superintendent of Pilotage, and a First Class Pilot. Each committee member would ask questions relative to his position with the principal examiner being the pilot. The examination would last for about an hour, covering subjects such as the courses to steer and distances to run in the navigating channel, the character of every buoy's flashing light, the sand banks and shoal waters, the candidate's knowledge of the International Rules and Regulations for navigating at sea, and lastly the local rules and regulations for navigating within the Port of Liverpool. Knowledge of all the lighthouses within the pilotage district was also included and candidates had to reach a standard equivalent to the examination for a third-class pilot's licence by the end of their apprenticeship. The average timespan from junior lad to a pilot's licence was six years, but promotion only came when a serving pilot retired or died. So, to begin with, it just was not worth thinking about it but to just get on with the job you were doing and wait for a new recruit to take your place and hope that he might stick it. My turn duly came, and I welcomed the new recruit who was obviously much smarter than me as he brought with him his own packet of "Flash" which was the latest floor cleaning product and worked twice as fast as Howard Baker soap. To my surprise, he was not banned from using it as some of the senior lads in the Service were of the old school who didn't believe in an easier life. My second pleasant surprise was that he didn't resign, which meant I was at last free of the chores of junior lad and could spend more time in the open air working on deck with the other apprentices. I was also picking up on the job of the bow lad in the punt and managing to keep clear of the lifting block once it was engaged. I also remembered to release the safety strop and to ship the plugs before cranking up the diesel engine prior to the arrival of the coxswain. Turning the engine over in the freezing cold using a starting handle was never easy, and there was always the danger that it might kick back and catch you on the rebound. Some boat hands had finished up with broken thumbs as a result, and the advice given was to keep thumb and fingers all on the upper side of the handle. I have to say that that was one of the jobs that I least liked, but fortunately I managed to scrape through without penalties and settled into the life of chart room lad. One of the pilot masters - a man called Joe Flewitt who was fat and completely bald was a particularly fussy and bullying individual who seemed to take pleasure in finding fault with just about everything that a boat hand did. On one occasion, when presented with a cup of tea whilst standing on the bridge wing, he threw the cup over the side and admonished the boat hand who had brought it saying "This tea is too cold laddie! Now go back and do it properly. I want you to scald the cup, scald the saucer and scald the spoon!" The boat hand then went back to the galley and did what he was told quite literally. The cup was glowing hot and was too hot to hold so he carried it on a tray back to the bridge. In the darkness of the wheelhouse Captain Flewitt snatched the cup from off the tray and took a large gulp from it. Some people claim that the cup stuck to his bottom lip, though this was never verified, but it did however suffice to keep Captain Flewitt quiet for a considerable time thereafter. Flewitt was a stickler for cleanliness and as it was my job to keep his and the other master's room clean and to make their beds each night. I had to be doubly sure that everything was scrupulously clean. He even insisted on having the toilet seat polished before he would use it. It was a source of amazement to me that he was still alive after hearing stories of the concoctions that people took up to him on the bridge in the name of a cuppa. But live on he did, to confound all predictions. Maybe caustic is a secret ingredient for longevity.

The life of an apprentice was governed by a four-week cycle which commenced with sailing day. This was the day all boat hands hated as it meant a return to duty after a week at home enjoying the life ashore. It also meant a period of extra hard work as the pilot boat would be very dirty having spent a week in the dock with various shore-based personnel, performing repairs and overhauling the engines and electrical gear. The decks would be heavily soiled with oil and grime trodden in by the workers, and the white paintwork would also be covered in a black haze of soot particles from the polluted air of the docks. The apprentices would man the ropes on leaving the berth and traversing the lock, and again at Princes Landing Stage at Liverpool where they would tie up and wait for the arrival of the pilots. The system of manning of pilots for both the Bar and Lynas stations centred around the need for a daily complement of 10 pilots at Lynas and

6 pilots at the Bar. Both pilot boats would radio in each day, as to their needs for the following 24 hours, and the tender boat would sail from the Stage each day around noon with the requisite number of pilots to top up the complement. The first day of duty would be to act as the tender boat and carry the pilots out to the Mersey Bar, where we would transfer the pilots bound for Lynas to the Bar boat, who would then proceed westwards to Lynas. We would then take over duty of the Bar station for the next 7 days and the Bar boat would begin a week of tender duties running each day from Princes Landing Stage to the Bar, and then onwards to Point Lynas, topping up the daily complement of pilots on each station. On his return journey from Point Lynas, he would stop at the Bar and take off the pilots outward bound on the tide from the Liverpool ports which included Garston, Birkenhead and Eastham locks at the entrance to the Manchester Ship Canal. When the last one had been taken off he would then proceed to Liverpool where he would land them at the Pierhead on the waterfront.

Back on the Bar pilot boat, the task of cleaning went on all the first day with soojiing (washing) the white paintwork clean using Teepol (a detergent), polishing all the brass work on the bridge, and scrubbing the wooden decks with a strong caustic dope using wire brooms. Caution was necessary here as the caustic needed to be added slowly to the bucket of water as it was liable to flare up if added too quickly, and we were all cautioned to never try to add water to the caustic crystals as this would result in serious injury. Sea boots were also necessary as the caustic would burn through any other footwear. This work would be done whilst traversing the buoyed channel on the way out to the Mersey Bar which was 16 miles out to sea, and would continue until darkness fell. As chart room lad I was still on day work along with the junior lad, but the other apprentices were split into 2 watches of 4 hands in each watch. They worked a system of 4 hours on duty and 4 hours off duty and this would carry on right through the 3 weeks spent at sea and would finish on docking day. The 3 weeks at sea were broken up into 3 parts. The first week was on the Bar station, the second week on tender duty, and the third week spent cruising off Point Lynas off the coast of Anglesey a distance of 51 miles from Liverpool. Lynas was the principal boarding station for ships inward to Liverpool as it offered shelter from the prevailing westerly winds which could suddenly turn to gale force at very short notice, making boarding hazardous at the Bar station.

The main task of the Bar station was to deal with the many vessels outward bound from the different ports situated on the Mersey. In addition to Liverpool itself, there was Garston, Birkenhead, Bromborough, Tranmere, the Dingle Oil Jetties, and the locks at Eastham controlling the traffic to and from the Manchester Ship Canal. Liverpool itself boasted a 7-mile stretch of enclosed dockland, and with a tidal range of over 10 metres twice daily on spring tides it was a busy time for the boat hands ferrying the pilots to and from the numerous ships visiting the Mersey Ports. The Bar station would also deal with any inward vessels coming from the north, but in gale force winds would be forced to take shelter in the river and inward ships would have to be diverted to Point Lynas. Some of the smaller vessels which were frequent visitors to the Port would bring themselves up the channel with the assistance of the Port Operations controllers, who would track the vessel using radar.

Following a week spent at the Bar station we would then be relieved by the boat which had just finished its week in dock, and it would be our turn to witness the sour faces of their boat hands who had just lost the luxuries of shore life in exchange for another 3 weeks of pitching and tossing on the Irish Sea. We were somewhat more cheerful, as we were now about to spend the next week on tender duties where we would get a chance to see our girlfriends when we were tied up for the night alongside the landing stage at the Pierhead. The week spent on tender duty was somewhat more pleasant than the monotony of the Bar Station, albeit very busy. Each day around lunch time we would receive our complement of pilots who would first muster in the local tavern, which went by the name of The Pig And Whistle, and we would then proceed outward bound to Point Lynas and return to the landing stage either late that evening or in the early hours of the next morning, depending on the time of the tide. On one day of that particular week, we were allowed the luxury of a visit from our girlfriends who would walk along the landing stage and come on board with cakes and goodies for their loved one. It was an unwritten rule that any confectionary received must be shared amongst all the boat hands and the crime of "bunk-scoffing" would lead to serious sanctions if unearthed. It was during one of these conjugal visits that a serious rift occurred between Boo Boo and Bear, which was to have lasting consequences. Bear had invited his paramour Derreka to join him in a bit of slap and tickle in his cabin prior to sailing. On leaving the boat he was escorting her back along the landing stage to the exit barrier. Boo Boo had been painting up on the foredeck and was leaning over the rails and waving an old pair of knickers that he had rescued out of the rag bag which was a sack full of cloths used for cleaning. Fortunately, Derreka was very short sighted so was unable to see the offending underwear being waved by Boo Boo, but Bear's eyesight was razor sharp and instantly homed in on the large hole in the gusset, throwing him into a fit of rage hitherto unseen. He pushed Derreka to one side and raced back along the landing stage towards the gangway with the intention of murdering Boo Boo. Boo Boo instantly realised that he had gone that one step too far in baiting Bear and knew that he was in danger of his very existence should Bear catch up with him, and promptly scuttled off down the chain locker for refuge. It was a wise choice as Bear did not find him and Boo Boo was able to resurface some 24 hours later when Bear had finally cooled down. Such was life as a boat hand. Never a dull moment.

But progress was about to change my life as a boathand in a quite dramatic way. Two new 52-foot launches were purchased to replace the ageing William Clarke cutter and were built to transport pilots to and from the Bar station and also to board and take off pilots from vessels. These launches were twin screw-powered with Rolls Royce engines with a speed of 21 knots. and could carry up to 12 pilots. The two launches "Puffin" and "Petrel" were manned with officers from the port authority and crewed by two apprentices from the Pilot Service. One launch was available for duty, with the other in dock undergoing maintenance. I was despatched to serve as crew, along with one other apprentice, and for this period of time I would work from my home in Tranmere. It was a huge change from my life on board the pilot boats and I enjoyed every moment of my time spent there gaining much experience of the buoyed channels and the boarding and landing of pilots from their ships. However, all good

Puffin launch.

things have their ups and downs and the down for me literally came one winters night on December 12th, 1962. I joined the "Petrel" at 2000 that stormy night at Woodside Landing stage on the Birkenhead side of the river. The wind was blowing from the northwest creating a heavy swell in the river with flurries of snow creating visibility problems. There were even lumps of ice floating on the surface, it was that cold. The Bar pilot boat had left its station at the Mersey bar and was anchored in the river close to the Cammell Laird ship yard. The landing stage at Liverpool was fully occupied with tugs tied up for the night, as were the two stages on the west side of the river - both Wallasey and Woodside, with ferry boats which had suspended operations for the night due to the bad weather. With all berths occupied, there was no place for us to go, with the exception of Tranmere Oil Jetty which was undergoing refurbishment following earlier damage. A decision was taken to head over to the oil jetty with a view to seeing if we could moor there for the night. It was pitch dark and the launch's searchlight was used to illuminate the landing area. I was despatched with a head rope in one hand to see if I could find a suitable place to make it fast. The area was slippery, so I proceeded with caution, but unbeknown to me the beam of timber that I was standing on came to an abrupt end and I stepped out into space. The next thing I remember was being underwater and fighting to get back to the surface. I was fully dressed in my uniform jacket which became heavy when wet and made it more difficult to break surface. The next moment, I am once more breathing fresh air and realising what has happened. The adrenalin has now kicked in and my principal aim is to get myself out onto dry land again. To this day I do not know how I did it, but I somehow got myself out and back onto the beam I had been on before. I could see the searchlight from the launch, which was scanning the river looking for me, but after a fruitless search returned to the jetty where they found me waiting. I was taken back aboard and transferred to the Bar pilot boat where I took a hot bath and was fed a large glass of whiskey and given a bed for the night whilst my clothes were dried out. That seemed to be the standard procedure in the Pilot Service for anyone who had suffered immersion. I went home to Tranmere and put the incident out of my mind, but two days later I suffered the aftereffects of shock and immersion and was bedridden for 24 hours, after which I thought I was now fully recovered. Unfortunately, it wasn't the case and some weeks later I developed problems with my lung which manifested itself as a shadow on an X ray examination. It was the start of a year of ill health resulting in spells of 3-month periods spent in a chest hospital with suspected TB. Following a private consultation with a Liverpool chest specialist based in Rodney Street who had experienced war time merchant seafaring casualties, he diagnosed that I had inhaled a foreign body into my lung, probably oil, during my period of immersion at Tranmere Oil Jetty and recommended that I undergo an operation to have it removed. This I willingly did as I was now seriously worried that my career as a Liverpool Pilot was in jeopardy. I had the surgery at Aintree Hospital in Liverpool and 6 weeks later was back to duties aboard Number 3 Pilot boat "Arnet Robinson". I served out the remaining part of my apprenticeship which involved trips with licenced pilots to all the different river entrances situated on the Mersey, which included the entrance to the Manchester Ship Canal at Eastham. I patiently awaited the news of a retirement that would lead to my invitation to join the elite ranks of Mersey Pilots. The call to the colours duly came in May 1966 and I presented myself at the Pilot office for examination to Pilot of the 3rd Class. This was the exact same building where I had stood those 8 years earlier as a 16-year-old with knocking knees in 1958. This time my knees were knocking even more as I faced the numerous questions put to me about my knowledge of how I would bring a ship up through the channels and sand banks, and how I would dock into and out of the numerous river entrances, and finally take it through the complex dock system to where it would finally be berthed ready to unload its cargo. The examination lasted an hour and a half, after which I was asked to leave the room whilst my fate was decided by the different examiners. It was with much relief, followed by great joy, that I was informed that I had been successful, and I should call back to the office the following day to collect my 3rd class licence. This I duly did and was despatched that same day to take out a coaster from the Port Of Garston in the south river. My licence restricted me to vessels of less than 600 tons and I spent the next 2 years learning my trade in all kinds of weather, during the hours of daylight, at night-time, in thick fog, and in heavy rainstorms. It was a huge learning curve, but the times were very exciting.

CHAPTER FIVE:
LIFE AS A THIRD CLASS PILOT

1966 was a very special year for me. England won the World Cup for the first and so far, only time. My team Everton won the FA Cup in a thrilling match V Sheffield Wednesday when I was still an apprentice, and I watched the game from the mess room on a black and white television which kept losing the picture every time the pilot boat closed on a vessel to be boarded. But most importantly it was the year that I finally joined the ranks of the licenced pilots. It was a sea change of lifestyle in the true sense of the word. From being a

Dave Devey: 1966.

nondescript employee of the Mersey Docks And Harbour Company as a boat hand, to the status of a self-employed Liverpool Pilot of the third class, was a huge change in my lifestyle. I swapped the ill-fitting uniform of a boat hand for a smart navy-blue suit, a white shirt and collar and tie, and was welcomed into the saloon by my fellow pilots who congratulated me on my accession to the fold. It was a totally different world to the one I had experienced those previous eight years and it took a while for me to realise that it had actually happened. I had previously attended the pilot office to collect my licence of the third class, which was a beautiful white vellum document which folded into a neat square with instructions to carry it at all times when on duty and to produce it when on board ship if asked by the ship's master. It was not a surprising thing to do as I was going aboard ships as a twenty-four-year-old pilot, where quite often the master was expecting to meet a much older person. It was also useful as an alternative to a passport, as in bad weather and outward bound from Liverpool, a pilot could be carried away to a foreign port if he is unable to disembark at the pilot station. There was an alternative to finishing up at a foreign port, and that was to head for Dunmore East on the east coast of Ireland. We had an arrangement with their pilots that they would take us off and land us at their pilot station. The Irish are a very hospitable nation, as anyone who has ever been to Ireland would vouch, so it was a much more pleasant alternative than pounding down the Irish Sea and maybe even the Bay of Biscay. One of the more senior pilots would tell us how he ended up in New York during the war armed only with a toothbrush, but I digress. My first job on becoming licenced was to apply to the GPO (General Post Office) to have a telephone installed in my home. This may seem a bit strange, but in those days a lot of people didn't have a phone and needed to be placed on a waiting list in order to get one. Pilots were seen as a priority profession and when asked for, were provided with one quickly. This was fortunate for me as my life would now be spent hanging on the end of a phone waiting to be given my next duty. The hub of the administration was based in the pilot office which is a red brick building situated on Canning river wall just south of the Liverpool Pierhead. The shore master was king of everything he surveyed here, and his job was to allocate pilots to the numerous vessels, both inward and outward, that were in request of one. He was viewed as God incarnate by the more junior pilots, who lived in fear of his wroth should you be late in ringing in for your allocated duty. I still have the occasional nightmare to this day in which I have forgotten to ring into the office for my ship and I now have to face a bollocking, and maybe even the sanction of the loss of a day's pay as a result. My nightmare was further impounded by the fact that I was away from home and had forgotten what his phone number was, and the longer I searched for it, the later it got. I am 78 years old and still occasionally wake up following this nightmare.

Many years later, the harbour authority told us that the building was unsafe and was about to collapse into the river. We had to move, lock stock and barrel, into the Mersey Docks And Harbour Company building, which constituted the southernmost of the 'Three Graces' situated at the Liverpool Pierhead. It was the first step in our subsequent path later on to oblivion as a self-employed independent group. More of that in later chapters. The pilot office still stands today and houses part of the Maritime Museum of Liverpool where the former pilot boat number 2 'Edmund Gardner' lies in her final resting place in the adjacent dry dock. I spent four of my six years apprenticeship on board that vessel with mostly happy memories. She is now one of the museum's attractions, and the public are given guided tours of her on selected occasions depicting what life was like on board at that time. The cruising pilot boats were phased out in the 1980's and replaced by high-speed launches, which are the current means of transporting todays' pilots out to, and back from the Mersey Bar some 16 miles from Liverpool.

Edmund Garnier.

1966 was also a significant year in the history of the Liverpool Pilot Service as it marked 200 years since the inception of the service as a body of amalgamated pilots, with each holding a share in the company. Prior to that time, pilots were independent groups with each owning and crewing their own sailing cutter. There were as many as 12 different boats, each plying its trade in trying to be first to board an inward bound vessel to the port. They were unlicenced and usually had previously been fishermen. It was a difficult and dangerous occupation, and many vessels became stranded on the numerous sand banks in the approaches to Liverpool, and subsequently were lost with all hands. This situation was untenable, and the Liverpool merchants complained to the government at their losses, which subsequently led to the legislation that created the first Liverpool Pilot Service in 1766. This brought in new regulations and the examination of pilots and the subsequent licencing of successful applicants. The loss of vessels dramatically lessened, and the Liverpool Pilot Service was born.

So, in 1966 it was decided to celebrate the occasion, and a grand dinner and ball was organised at the Adelphi Hotel for those pilots and their partners who were free of duty on that night. The Adelphi at that time was the most prestigious hotel in Liverpool, which has sadly since gone into decline. I was pilot number 180 and was the second most junior pilot of the whole assembly. It was awe inspiring seeing so many diverse people all beautifully dressed, and the grandeur of the occasion still sticks in my mind to this day. The pilot service was at its peak. The eleven miles of dockland on the Liverpool side of the river was full of ships of all classes and sizes. The Manchester Ship Canal was also busy, as was Birkenhead, Bromborough, and Garston. This gave to the new pilot a huge variety of experience, and again, a steep learning curve was required to take on board all the vagaries of approaching and leaving each dock entrance. But it was exciting to be part of the big show which twice daily occurred with the approach of each high water, and on spring tides that could mean a rise and fall of over 10 metres or 32.5 feet if you're one of the old-school. The only other port in the country that has a bigger rise and fall is Bristol, with some 40 feet. In those days we calculated under keel clearance (the distance between the bottom of a vessel and the seabed) in feet and inches, and it was only when we joined the Common Market that we were obliged to start thinking in metres for the purposes of determining the draught of each vessel (the amount of ship that is below the water line and is therefore not visible). Some of the older pilots found it difficult to adapt to this new thinking as they had spent a lifetime working in feet and inches, but eventually converted to this European idea with a degree of reluctance. It is very important for the pilot to know precisely what this figure is, as they have to work with falling tides which could leave the ship stranded if they make a miscalculation. A pilot must always have a minimum of 2 feet (0.6 of a metre) underneath the ship in order to be safe and that has to go into their decision as to whether they can proceed or not with the task they have been given. They also have to take account of the "squat" of the vessel when proceeding in shallow water. Squat is the amount that the draught will increase when the vessel is moving, as it will increase proportionally with the ship's speed and will make the vessel go deeper in the water, usually by the bow as the speed increases. On a falling tide this could make the difference in the calculation as to whether to proceed or not.

Today's pilot carries a VHF (portable radio) which they use to communicate with the port control operator who will give them updates on the height of the tide from monitors situated at various stations in the main channel leading into the river itself, and the various locks where they will finally dock. The present port control building is situated on the northwest corner of Seaforth Dock and is operated 24 hours a day, similar to the airport control centres around the country. It is linked by radar to show the river and main channels, and their coverage extends as far westwards as Point Lynas in Anglesey. The port control will identify and monitor the movements of any vessels which come into their radar coverage and direct them to a point where they can be safely boarded by a pilot. When the pilot is on board, the port control can also keep him informed of any other vessels navigating the channel, which gives him an opportunity to speak with the pilot on the other vessel using his VHF where they can safely meet and pass each other. The pilot also has contact with the various locks situated on the river whose dock master can relay what is happening at the dock entrance in relation to the movement any vessel that might be outward bound. On the larger vessels which employ the use of tugs to assist in the docking, the pilot can also speak with the tug master as to how to make the best approach to the lock. The tug masters in Liverpool are very experienced personnel and are trained to read each situation as it presents itself with wind and tide the main factors and the pilot is there to oversee the whole operation. This will involve orders to the helmsman as to what course they should steer and latterly how much helm to put on in order to alter the direction of the ship. The pilot will also control the speed of the vessel by the use of the engines in both going ahead or in going astern when the need to stop the vessel is required. All in all, pilots are extremely busy when it comes to the final approach to the locks when the master of the vessel starts to become extremely apprehensive as to the final outcome of what looks like an impossible task. A frequently asked question at this point goes "Are you sure Mr. Pilot that my ship will fit in that lock? The pilot knows of course that it will because they have previously docked many other vessels of similar size into the same lock and a reassurance that it will is usually enough to placate the captain's nerves until their ship is safely moored in the lock. However, the pilot's job has not finished at the lock. When the outside gate is closed behind the ship, the lockmaster will open the inner paddles which will lift the vessel up to the level of the dock complex. The pilot then has to navigate it through the dock system and finally to its berth where it will be secured to the quay and the cargo can be discharged or loaded. Because of the large rise and fall of tide twice daily, Liverpool has an impounded dock system. A collision with the inside lock gates would be catastrophic should the gates part, which would result in the discharge of a large part of the dock system of its water into the river. This scenario did occur one time in the south docks when a vessels engines failed to go astern whilst approaching Brunswick Lock and it subsequently hit one of the inside gates which parted and drained a large area of the south docks of its water.

Brunswick Lock.

They eventually found the damaged gate some one mile away on the other side of the river. Amazingly nobody was injured on board the vessel in question, which belonged to the Isle Of Mann Steam Packet Company, which was washed out of the lock and totally out of control. So even touching a lock gate was viewed as a serious crime by the harbour authority and every pilot including myself tried to make sure it never happened to them. The use of tugs was also a safeguard in the event that the engines failed, and the tug made fast aft could use its power to bring the vessel to a halt.

But I'm jumping a bit ahead now so I must go back to 1966 when I held a third-class licence which limited me to vessels of 600 tons which would not normally employ a tug. And furthermore, the aids to navigation that I have just mentioned did not exist when I got my licence, when fog was a frequent occurrence in those days. It usually manifested itself around the hour of seven in the morning and lasted till about ten or eleven when the heat from the sun would finally disperse it. This almost daily phenomenon was caused by the simultaneous lighting of lounge fires in the numerous houses adjoining the river when the public arose from their nights' slumber. Most houses were heated by a coal burning fire which created a fair amount of smoke and served to give pilots navigating the channel further headaches, as radar sets were very much in their infancy or quite often didn't exist on a lot of vessels. Decisions to proceed or not depended on the visibility reports which other pilots with a workable radar set would relay back as they made progress through the dredged channels. The 2 main channels - the Queens and Crosby, were flanked with stone walls which were built to keep out the siltation which was carried in with the tide. Dredgers were employed to maintain the depth of the channel to a minimum depth of 6.8 metres at low water. Every pilot's nightmare is, that having taken the decision to proceed, the visibility would drop to zero at which point it was impossible to turn back and with a flood tide pushing them ever onwards. This is when the pilot comes into his own and now needs every skill he has ever learned to get that vessel safely up the channel, and subsequently into a lock which is scarcely wider than the ship. The channel has a large bend in it and the pilot would have to navigate blind just using the courses to steer between each buoy which he has implanted in his memory from a very early age. My job as a third-class pilot was to make sure I kept well out of the way of the larger vessels and gave them sufficient room to manoeuvre in safety. As a junior pilot you lived in a kind of admiration and sometimes awe of the elder brethren who were handling the very largest ships which visited the port. Seniority was hugely important in the Service, which continued through from the apprenticeship days, and when gathered in the saloon of the pilot boat you only spoke when you were spoken to. The outward-bound pilots who had been taken off their ships via a rope ladder and a trip in the punt care of the apprentices, were obliged to wait until the daily tender boat returned from its round trip to the Point Lynas station boat. This could mean a wait of some six hours, with another hour and a half on the tender boat back to Liverpool. To pass the time, there was invariably a card school and a discussion group who reminisced about their past adventures, accompanied by a glass of whisky care of a satisfied master or "happy cappy" in local parlance. It was the custom of ships' masters to show their appreciation for a job well done i.e., no damage to his ship, by a gift of a bottle of spirits which was usually Johnny Walker Red Label whisky. This would not escape the attentions of those who were waiting in anticipation of a drop of sustenance to help while away the many hours spent captive. The net result was a lively discussion which centred around previous near catastrophes that had befallen fellow colleagues whilst on board and navigating their ships. This was hugely important to the junior pilots who learnt from these conversations of some of the perils experienced by their more senior mentors.

CHAPTER SIX:
LIFE AS A SECOND CLASS PILOT

The two years spent as a Third Class Pilot flew by and I soon had to prepare for my second-class licence, which again was held at the red stone pilot office on Canning river wall. The fear and trepidation which I experienced for my third-class licence had almost disappeared, but I still faced the committee with a degree of cautious apprehension as to what questions I would be asked. The main examiner was a senior pilot who concentrated mostly on how I would deploy my tugs when negotiating the various river entrances. I must have satisfied him with my limited knowledge of something which I still hadn't yet done, which was to use tugs, as he credited me with a pass, and I became a Second Class Pilot and licenced to pilot vessels of up to 2,000 tons gross. This was a big step for me as the vessels were considerably larger with some requiring towage. In those days the means of communication between pilot and tug master was a pea whistle to the head tug and the ship's own whistle to the stern tug. The various signals were one long blast followed by three short blasts to pull to starboard and one long blast followed by two short blasts to pull to port and one short blast to stop pulling. Short wave radios were in their infancy in those days and only came into usage many years later and are now today's tool for the modern day pilot to communicate with his tugs. The system was subject to flaws, especially in strong cross winds when the head tug was having difficulty in hearing the pea whistle signals, but as I said previously the tug masters were extremely experienced and frequently anticipated the direction in which to tow that was needed to keep the ship safe.

Dave Devey 1968.

I have two vivid memories of my time as a Second Class Pilot one of which was pleasant and the other the stuff of nightmares. The latter one involved a Russian vessel called the "Irtysh" which was built in 1917 with the bridge amidships and the decks stacked high with

The Irtysh by Wolfgang Fricke.

timber from Vladivostok. So high was the timber that you needed platform shoes to be able to see over it and as a consequence which way you were heading. I managed by standing on tip toe and we proceeded into the main channel. The ship was so old that it was steered by two chains which ran from the wheel down the scuppers on each side of the ship finishing at the rudder. To compound the problem the wind was blowing from the northwest and very strong at force seven on the Beaufort scale. The direction of this wind is particularly bad for Liverpool Bay as it offers no shelter to vessels navigating the channels and creates a swell in the river. A further problem was the stability of the "Irtysh" being top heavy, with the deck timber soaking up a lot of water and the fuel tanks half empty. This caused the vessel to heel over from one side to the other making it very difficult to maintain a course to steer. The main channel has a large bend to starboard (right) at the halfway stage and has retaining walls on each side. It was here that the trouble started. At certain points in the turn I started to doubt if she would make it, as the wheel was hard over to starboard and she was still going straight with the wall dead ahead. Right at the last minute she started to turn, and then it was necessary to get the wheel back to midships (centre) and then hard over to port (left) to stop the swing. We somehow managed to negotiate the bend and were now on a straight stretch. Another vessel called the "Mansoor", a Pakistani vessel of some 15, 000 tons deadweight approached from behind and made to overtake us passing down our port side. Just at this moment the "Irtysh took a wicked swing to port and the Russian quartermaster shouted in Russian indicating he had lost control by a shrug of his shoulders. I ordered him to put the wheel hard to starboard and the engines to full astern and to let go the starboard anchor. All these things were of no use, and we collided with the Mansoor's starboard side as she was passing us. Our port anchor was still in its housing and the flukes buried themselves in the other ship's side, opening it up just as though it

The Mansoor.

was a tin opener. We bounced back off the Mansoor, which disappeared into the darkness which had now fallen, leaving us swinging to a starboard anchor in the Crosby channel. Looking back on it, we were very lucky that it hadn't happened some minutes earlier as we would then have found ourselves beam on and under the bow of the Mansoor with a very much different result. As it was, there were no casualties on either ship and the subsequent enquiry cleared me of any blame, but it was certainly a wakeup call as to what can happen so suddenly and with little or no warning.

On the other side of the fence, life as a pilot can be sometimes very rewarding, as was my experience with Her Majesty's submarine "Osiris". Again strangely enough, the wind was blowing strongly from the northwest and as I said before, it offers no shelter in

HMS Osiris.

Liverpool Bay as it is blowing directly into the mouth of the Mersey River. Boarding a ship in this weather can be quite daunting but boarding a submarine is something again. It was a Friday afternoon in late November and was particularly significant for the crew as they were scheduled for a weekend furlough in Birkenhead Docks. My first problem was how to get aboard. There was no rope ladder as is normally the case, but there were half-moon shaped steps cut into the hull of the submarine which were situated close to the bow (front). This created a swell with the seas pouring over the entire ship and I had a number of attempts at boarding with the punt riding three or four feet up and down the curved shaped hull. At last, I saw my chance and leapt for the steps and scurried up onto the deck before the punt followed me. I was grabbed by a rather large hairy-arsed matelot who apologised for the lack of a safety rail as he said the weather was too bad to rig one! He kept tight hold of me as we made our way aft to the conning tower as the seas were breaking over the hull and cascading over the lee side. I was completely wet through by the time I arrived at the conning tower and was warmly greeted by the commander who took me down to his cabin and presented me with a new set of clothes, whilst a steward took away my wet ones. I explained to the commander that time was pressing and that it was touch and go if we would be able to dock on this tide. So off we went at maximum speed and headed up the channel bound for Birkenhead. The commander explained how important it was that we made that tide as the town dignitaries were already booked to visit on arrival that evening, and a celebration dinner had been arranged in their honour. This was clearly a case of pulling all the stops out to facilitate the best possible chance of us making that tide. We made good time up the channel and arrived off Birkenhead, where two tugs were awaiting to assist us through the river entrance and into the basin where we would be lifted up to the same level as the dock and then proceed to the berth.

At this point I realised that we would not have enough time to make the tugs fast, as it was now close to high water, and it would not be possible to dock on the ebb (falling) tide. I briefly explained to the commander that I was intending to proceed without tug assistance, and he said that if I felt it was safe enough, then to keep on going. We proceeded through the lock and into the basin where we made fast, to the delight of the crew. A frogman duly arrived on the bridge and said "Everything fine, sir!" and when I enquired of the commander his purpose for saying that, he explained that the submarine had very sensitive equipment below the waterline which needed checking as a precaution. Once we were in the berth and all fast it was party time, and I was invited to join the officers in the wardroom where they made a fuss of me and thanked me for my efforts in getting them in. My clothes duly arrived all clean and freshly pressed, and I was able to return home as though nothing had happened. By a strange quirk of fate, some ten years later I was assigned to a Leander-class frigate which was due to proceed to sea from Alexandra Dock in Liverpool. On joining, I introduced myself to the commanding officer who said to me "I remember you pilot, from when I was Number One on the Osiris." He was sitting in his usual leather chair looking slightly jaded and he said, "Had a bit of a do at the town hall in Manchester last night, so could you just carry on while I watch?" I was very happy to do that and took extra care to make sure that we didn't scrape the paintwork. Sometimes the world can be a very small place!

My three years spent as a Second Class Pilot were hugely important in learning the ways of handling ships under towage. The tug masters in Liverpool are highly skilled and for the most part will anticipate the needs of the pilot in advance of his asking, but at the end

Tug boats in Liverpool by Niels Johannes.

of the day there has to be an overall controller of the whole operation, and that falls to the pilot. In the final approaches to the dock entrance, the pilot must gauge their speed using the ships engines, so as to make the tugs fast safely - too much speed and the tug cannot give their towing wire to the ship's crew. The pilot must give precise orders to the helmsman to make the ship go in the intended direction, and they must keep in contact with both the Port Control Centre and the dock master using their hand-held VHF radio. They must use all of these skills in order to arrive off the lock entrance at the time they have been allotted for docking, whilst making sure that the vessel keeps in sufficient water to be able to maintain an under keel clearance of 0.6 metres (2 feet), and whilst liaising by radio with other vessels using the main navigation channels. What does make my blood boil however, is the UK government's conception of what exactly a pilot does. They are convinced that the pilot is merely an adviser to the master of the vessel and that the master brings their own ship in and out of port. Nothing could be further from the truth, and I can say with hand on heart that in my 40 years and 4 months as a licenced and then authorised pilot, I never experienced one single master who might even be remotely interested in trying to take over the con of the vessel from my charge. Considering that Great Britain is an island which is dependent for 95% of its goods by way of shipping, I am constantly in despair of the behaviour of UK government officials towards the pilotage profession. I myself have personal experience of this unseemly attitude, but that is for a later chapter.

The gap between Second Class and First Class is immense. From being limited to vessels of 2000 tons as a Second Class Pilot, the sky is now the limit. Following yet another visit to the pilot office for examination by the committee and having produced the requisite number of 'leadsmans' (certificates obtained following visits to all the dock entrances in the company of a First Class Pilot), I passed my final examination and became a First Class Pilot. This to me was my crowning achievement, I had finally made it.

CHAPTER SEVEN:
LIFE AS A FIRST CLASS PILOT

The year is 1971 and at long last I had achieved my goal of becoming a First Class Pilot. No more exams - ever! But the learning curve had now gone crescent shaped, and the responsibilities became that much greater. The ships were much longer and wider, and of course deeper than before, but the dock entrances still remained the same size. All the experience that I had gained in my formative years as a junior pilot was now needed to cope with my new change of status. For a pilot there is no hiding place and once given a task to

Dave Devey 1971.

perform, the execution of it rests in his own hands. There may be a brief period before boarding the ship when he can ask for advice from a more experienced colleague about the problems he might duly face, but once on-board decisions have to be taken and acted upon solely by the pilot himself without consultation with anyone else. In many cases the master of the vessel may never have visited the port before and is unfamiliar with the procedures necessary in safely navigating the channels and negotiating the dock entrances. They are only too happy to hand over the whole responsibility of the berthing procedure to the pilot himself, who will outline their own intentions and give times of importance of the passage including when they are scheduled to enter the lock. Communication can also present a problem for the pilot. My own experience of the language difficulties that sometimes arise was when I had been boarded a large Chinese bulker that was bound for Liverpool docks to pick up scrap iron, and the Chinese captain approached me with quite an anxious expression on his face. "Ot tie grasser rock?" he shouted at me. I puzzled for a moment, but was unable to understand what he meant. "Sorry but I no understand" I replied in my best pidgin English. "Please tell me again." "OT TIE GRASSER ROCK!", he repeated even louder, and angry that I could not understand what he thought was perfect English. My lack of understanding would also be seen as a loss of face by the captain with a large crowd of crew members gathered on the bridge, who were eating raw duck eggs from a wicker basket. When I shrugged my shoulders to indicate that I still didn't know what he meant he became very agitated and gestured at the chart of the river which was set out on the chart table and pointing at Gladstone Lock, which is where we were due to dock. At last, I could piece together what he was saying when I realised that Grasser Rock was Gladstone Lock and therefore the first bit must be "What time?" These things are made to try you. Once I had translated his request and given him the answer, he became more relaxed and was even delighted when we had safely encountered the locks and dock system and were all fast on the berth. One could almost say that he ended up a very 'happy---- scrappy----- cappy!'

Modern day pilotage requires the pilot to give to the master on boarding the ship a written passage plan describing every detail of his intentions, but that was not the case in my time. A lot of people think that the captain brings in his own ship and the pilot is merely an advisor. That is simply not the case and government ministers have been persuaded of this argument and as a consequence, the status of the majority of employed pilots in the UK has been downgraded. For an island nation that is mostly dependent on shipping for its existence, this is an ongoing scandal.

One of the things that came to irk me as I settled into the daily routine of a First Class Pilot was the system of appropriation which operated at Liverpool. Some pilots were appropriated to a particular shipping line and were paid an additional sum of money as a retainer fee, the details of which were not disclosed. They could also earn additional fees for manoeuvring a vessel within the enclosed dock system at Liverpool - which was outside the pilotage district (which finished at the lock entrance). Their earnings were a close kept secret from their colleagues who were designated 'rota pilots'. The appropriated pilots were known as "steam men" which originated from the advent of the steam ship in competition with the sailing vessels at the turn of the century. The system was extremely divisive and led to bad feeling between the two different factions. One particular practice which further highlighted the unrest was the manner of their appointment. There was no advertisement for the vacant post and as a result no interviews in which to select the most suitable candidate. The appointment was simply announced as a 'fait acomplis' with no explanation as to why that particular person had been chosen. Suspicion fell on the secretive practices of the masonic fraternity, but it was frequently difficult to identify who was and who wasn't a mason. All attempts to end the practice resulted in failure and it was still active right up to 1997 when all earnings were pooled and all pilots were able to retire on the same pension as their fellow colleagues. But that story is for another chapter.

Despite the atmosphere created by the divisive system which was ever present, along with the hope that one day it would all change and everybody could share in the abundance and variety of ships that visited the river each day, life as a Liverpool Pilot was very satisfying. But sadly, like all good things, status quo began to change, and our way of life came to an end, not with a bang, but more of a whimper. The number of ships visiting the port went into decline following our decision to join the European Common Market, and trade dramatically switched to the east coast ports such as Hull and Felixstowe. The advent of the container ship was also seen as a major factor in the port's decline. As a group of self-employed men, we were obliged to share the pool of money (appropriation excepted) equally, dependent on the class of licence held. With less ships, the pool became ever smaller month by month, until it was decided that action had to be taken to alleviate the lost revenue. This came in the form of a declaration from the elected representatives that the Pilot Service would allow a number of pilots to temporarily leave Liverpool on secondment and pilot ships in other ports for a period of up to 2 years. This would give the remaining pilots a greater share of the pool. The year was 1977 and was the turning point which marked the end of that happy life that I had earlier enjoyed, and heralded the beginnings of a new and very different way of life.

PILOT OF THE FIRST CLASS

No. 136

PORT OF LIVERPOOL

PILOT'S LICENCE

FOR THE

LIVERPOOL PILOTAGE DISTRICT.

To all to whom these presents shall come.

The Mersey Docks and Harbour Company, being the Pilotage Authority for the Liverpool Pilotage District, send greeting.

Know ye that .... DAVID DEVEY ....
aged 37 years, being 5 feet 10½ inches in stature, having a FRESH complexion, and whose place of abode is 19 MILL LANE, GAYTON, WIRRAL, having in pursuance of the provisions of the Pilotage Act, 1913, the Liverpool Pilotage Order, 1920, and the Liverpool Pilotage Bye-Laws, and all other powers us enabling, been duly examined on our behalf, and found to be qualified to act as a Pilot for shipping within the Liverpool Pilotage District, is, by this our Certificate, duly licensed to act as a *Pilot of the First Class* for the Liverpool Pilotage District, as defined in the Liverpool Pilotage Order, 1920, from the date hereof until the first day of December, 1980, provided that he shall so long comply with the provisions of the said Act and Order, and of all other Acts and Orders binding upon him in relation to Pilotage, and with every Order, Bye-Law or Regulation made by us, the said Company, and shall conduct himself with propriety and prudence.

Given by the said Mersey Docks and Harbour Company under the hand of their Secretary, this First day of December, in the year of our Lord One thousand Nine hundred and Seventy nine.

for Secretary.

Dave Devey: First Class Licence.

CHAPTER EIGHT: LIFE IN THE REPUBLIC OF GUINEA

A number of pilots took up this offer including myself, and I applied for a post in The Republic Of Guinea in West Africa. I hadn't a clue as to which Guinea it was as there are more than one, and it was after studying the map of Africa that I discovered that it was a former French Colony and that a communist led insurrection had forced the French out and had set up a government headed by Secou Toure. The port I was being seconded to was called Port Kamsar, which had recently been built to accommodate the bulk vessels that were needed to ship out the rich seams of bauxite being mined by the consortium of Alcan Alcoa based in Pittsberg, Pensylvania. Guinea is rich in this orangey-red mineral ore from which aluminium is produced and has a high content of ore per ton of earth mined.

When I applied for this post, I was interviewed at the Adelphi Hotel in Liverpool (yes, the same hotel I mentioned when I attended the bicentenary party as a newly fledged pilot in 1966) by a Brit by the name of Martial Chalmers who was working out in Port Kamsar as buoy master. I heard no more from him as to whether or not I had met the company's criteria for the position, so I continued to pilot in Liverpool. Totally out of the blue, I got a phone call to ask me how soon I could arrive in Kamsar. I was a bit taken aback by the suddenness of the invitation and said that I needed to consult my wife. I was given 24 hours in which to make up my mind and within that period we made a decision to give it a go. As part of the preparations for departure we visited the Liverpool School Of Tropical Medicine and the doctor Andrew Semple, who gave us our various jabs which were required for that country said "Are you sure you want to go to Guinea as it is considered one of the countries with the highest rate of tropical diseases?" That did nothing to boost my confidence, but we were already committed to leaving as we had rented our house to tenants and were booked on a Belgian Airways Sabena flight to Conakry, along with our two children, Andrew aged 5, and James aged 3. Little did I know it at the time, but I was to be reacquainted with the Liverpool School Of Tropical Medicine following the termination of my contract with Alcan Alcoa, but this time as a patient. Read on…

We had "burnt our boats" so to speak and were about to start a new chapter in our lives, which would fundamentally change all of us in our perception of the world and its people. For me, I had already experienced other cultures in my time spent at sea with Blue Funnel Line, but even with that knowledge, it still didn't stop me from being apprehensive about the whole venture. I told myself the two boys would be excited to be going to live in a foreign country with a chance to learn French, as that was the national language of The Republic of Guinea. My wife Pat was philosophical about the whole idea, but kept her thoughts to herself about what she really felt about the whole thing.

We arrived at Conakry, the capital of Guinea, and stepped out into the blazing heat of a typical African day and were escorted to the company's hostel where we would spend the next three days awaiting our transport

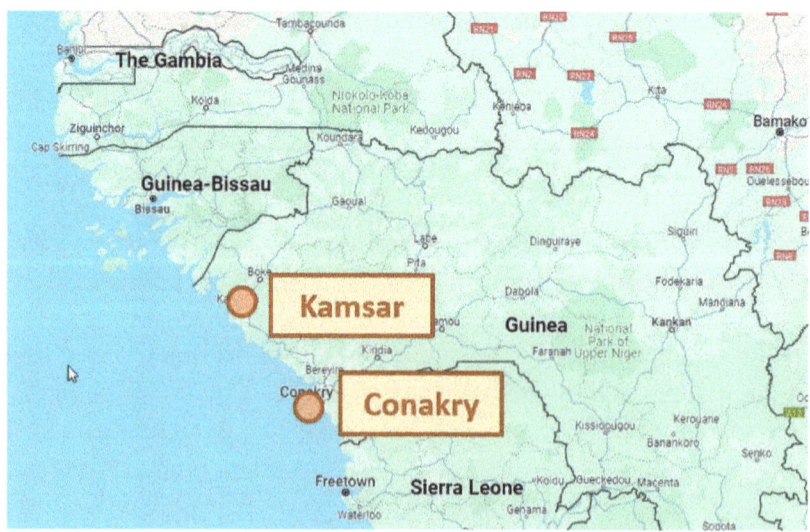

The Republic of Guinea.

onwards to the living quarters at Kamsar. The plane when it arrived was a Guinean Airways Dakota which had been requisitioned but from the second world war and refurbished with wooden seating for the passengers. We managed to squeeze into a tight space as more and more Guineans climbed aboard with all their animals that they had bought in the market in Conakry. It looked more like Noah's ark, as there seemed to be two of every living thing. I noticed that most of the local people wear wearing heavy overcoats and one lady even had a fur coat. I thought that a bit odd considering the sweltering heat but thought that maybe they had bought the clothes at the market in Conakry and were saving baggage room. On hearing the engines rev up I told everyone to buckle up as we were about to take off. We all looked for our seat belts in vain to discover that they had been cut off some long time ago and no longer existed. I imagined that they were probably holding someone's trousers up by now, but I didn't have time to dwell on it as we laboured down the runway with the engines at full throttle. One or two Muslim passengers were in deep supplication to the above, which made me even more apprehensive. We eventually left the ground after what seemed an interminable time and soared into the blue skies. It was only then that I realised why everybody was overdressed. Whilst we were ascending through the cloud base, the temperature in the cabin suddenly dropped and large wisps of cloud vapour began to swirl into the cabin. Now it was us Brits that were all under-dressed in our summer rigs and we spent the next half hour with teeth chattering until we finally arrived at our destination of Kamsar Village.

The houses were listed A to D in order of the perceived status of the employee within the Company. We were allotted a C house and the use of a Volkswagen beetle car, which was needed as a means of transport to the bauxite jetty where the bulk cargo vessels were moored some 1 mile distant from where we were based. They were all single-story buildings and furnished in a Swedish style and provided with air conditioning, which unfortunately wasn't the case with the beetle which only had an air blowing system which pumped out hot air. As a result, the car would double as an oven during the heat of the day and should you dare try to sit in without first placing a towel on the seat, you could end up with third degree burn marks on your back and buttocks. But in its favour, it did actually float on water as my wife and I discovered one day when we were faced with what looked like a large lake blocking our path on the road to Boke, where we were heading to collect our monthly issue of the local currency aptly named 'Sylis'. These Sylis were almost worthless in currency value outside of Guinea, but were needed to pay the wages of the house boys who were employed to look after the ex-pats' living accommodation. On our way to Boke that day, a couple of weeks after we had arrived, we had our first experience of life in the raw in the Republic Of Guinea. We were approaching a bend in the newly tarmacked road (the only one I ever saw in the whole of Guinea outside of Conakry) when we came to a traffic jam. To me, this was an enigma as there were very few cars on the roads at that time. We were soon to find out why. No sooner had we stopped when a man arrived on the scene and started hammering on my window. We thought that we were being robbed and sat in the car with the doors locked. When he started shouting "Au secours!" and pointing to the railway embankment we realised something was seriously wrong and jumped out of the car. He grabbed hold of my arm and pulled me towards what turned out to be the railway line. We climbed down the steep embankment and on to the track where we were met with the sight of a huge engine and all its waggons loaded with bauxite stopped on the tracks. We proceeded to walk towards the train, when I saw what looked like a severed arm lying on the tracks and shortly afterwards a leg which had also been severed. We then realised what to expect and it was worse than we had anticipated. A man was lying between the rails, and he had lost both arms and both legs but was still alive. My wife Pat who was a trained nurse quickly took off her cotton top and tore it into strips which she used as tourniquets to arrest the bleeding. I noticed that she was kneeling with her legs across the track and close to one of the giant wheels. I cautioned her to change her position in case the train moved, and we would end up with two casualties and not one. When she had staunched all the bleeding, the local villagers approached with an open-backed waggon and reversed up to the casualty and lifted him onto the tail section. Shortly after this, he succumbed to his injuries and died on the back of the truck. A large crowd of villagers had gathered by now and the women started wailing his loss by vibrating their tongues, which made an eyrie lamenting sound. All this, and we had only been in Guinea a few weeks! We returned to the car and waited for the train to be moved as it was stopped on a level crossing. A relief driver was sent for as the first was too distressed and shocked to carry on. Eventually, the road was cleared and we proceeded to Boke where we visited a rather strange looking bank which had bat wing doors just like in the cowboy movies. I imagined how easy it would be to rob such a place, but later realised that it wouldn't be worth the bother. We were handed a wad of banknotes of various denominations and headed off back to Kamsar a little more worldly wise than when we had left. We were later told that the train accident was a frequent happening as the track was used by the older and sick Guineans as a means of ending their lives.

As I mentioned before, the Sylis were used to pay for the employment of a house boy. It was against my principles to have a servant, but we were persuaded of the argument that it was a form of much needed revenue for the local Guineans, so we relented and took Mamadu on probation. He lasted 3 months and was subsequently discharged when large quantities of household goods could not be accounted for. I was called to a tribunal held by the local officials and was made to pay compensation to Mamadu for his loss of earnings. I saw him again about a week later happy in the employ of another ex-pat, so he did quite well from the deal. The windows on all the houses were heavily barred to protect the occupants from intruders, which made one feel a little apprehensive when night arrived. Who were these so-called intruders? The Guineans, when asked, would say they are not local people but that they come from Sierra Leone. Guinea has borders with no less than six other countries namely Senegal, Mali, Sierra Leone, Ivory Coast, Liberia, and the neighbouring former Portuguese colony of Guinea Bissau which was situated just across the other side of the River Nunez from Port Kamsar. The Guineans themselves lived in the nearby "village" which was a typical African settlement of thatch-rooved houses where the crew members of the pilot launch resided. These two men would man the small launch which carried the pilot out some 12 nautical miles through the twisting buoyed channel to where the bulk carrier would be waiting and ready, to proceed to its berth where it would load some 60,000 tons of bright orange bauxite.

The bauxite would be shipped around the world to the different processing plants, which would then turn it into aluminium. This bauxite was mined in Sangredi and shipped by huge Canadian-built trains to the crushing and drying plant at Kamsar, where it would end up as a heavy orange sand-like product which could be loaded into the waiting bulker via a conveyor belt. The Jetty Superintendent was a dour Scotsman by the name of Ron Robb, whose boast was that he could load a ship at a rate of 2000 tons per hour, but in the two years in which I piloted them in and out of Kamsar I don't recollect him ever achieving that goal largely due to the fact that the conveyor belt frequently broke down.

Kamsar jetty with conveyor belts.

I very soon learned that life as a pilot here was totally different to the one I had left behind in Liverpool. There were other duties to perform in addition to handling the navigation of the ships, one of which involved computing the twice daily tides using an almanac of the tides in Freetown, Sierra Leone. It was a monthly task which necessitated calculating both the time of high water for each day, and the height of that tide which varied from day to day. This was crucial to the whole shipping part of the bauxite operation as it determined how much cargo could be loaded on any given day in that month. In addition to computing the tides each month, it was the pilot's duty to calculate what the height of tide would be at one hour before high water on the day a ship was scheduled to leave for sea, and what draft the ship could load to allowing for an underwater clearance of 0.6 of a metre. The sailing time of one hour before high water was deemed to be when the vessel would have the most water underneath it in order to safely navigate the buoyed channel through the sandbanks and out to deep waters some 11 miles out to sea. This passage would take about one and a half hours from the time of leaving, and with channel buoys the size of a Heinz bean can and with a candle power of about two glow worms on the job, it could be very difficult to navigate at night, especially if there was a swell running which could obliterate the light altogether. Another hazard facing a pilot when navigating the channel was that these buoys would drag from their position and even change places, so that a port-hand buoy became a starboard-hand buoy and vice- versa, and it was left to the pilot as to what he should do next when confronting a situation like that in the dead of night. This is when a pilot's instinct clicks in and he immediately realises that things are not what they should be and then has only minutes in which to make a decision, which if wrong, could result in the grounding of the ship in his charge and with a falling tide, even more serious consequences.

My time of arrival in Guinea coincided with the start of what I had been told was the "cricket season". In my naivety I thought to myself "I didn't know that the game of cricket was played in Guinea", but I realise now that I was discovering new things every day. I very soon found out what they meant a few days later when the skies suddenly turned black followed by a downpour of hundreds and thousands of large black crickets, most of which seemed to die where they landed. The whole ground turned black, and it was almost impossible to walk without treading on them. Eventually they were swept up by the locals and burned in large bonfires. This heralded the beginning of the rainy season which was to last for six weeks and served as a nightmare period for any kind of navigation. The wind would arrive without any warning, followed by torrential rain, and I mean torrential… I remember getting caught in the middle of one of these storms as I was approaching the bend in the channel on a 60,000-ton bulker and the visibility suddenly turned to zero with the rain hitting the bridge wing horizontally where I was standing, at about force 10 on the Beaufort scale. I judged the visibility by the fact that I could not see my hand as I stretched it out in front of me. Fortunately, these squalls only lasted about 10 minutes or so, but that was a long time when you were navigating blind, as the ship's radar screen resembled a rice pudding with no way of discerning what was or wasn't a channel buoy. Somehow or another I managed to survive these ordeals without the ship running aground and I became convinced that somebody up there must be looking after me.

My clothes would end up completely sodden and I had no option but to carry on until the ship was safely alongside the loading jetty. Approaching the jetty would involve a manoeuvre to port using the ship's anchor as there was no available tug strong enough to assist the 180 degree turn with the tide still flooding and pushing the vessel towards the approaching mud banks further upstream. Not an easy task with a bulker of some 60,000 tons and a captain who is close to a nervous breakdown. But in the 2 years that I was there I only had one captain who tried to interfere by moving the telegraph to "stop" at a crucial time that I needed the engines, and I was forced to read the riot act to him that if he did it again I would hand over the navigation to him. He didn't as it happened, and we were able to recover the situation and berth without damage. He turned out to be very proficient at playing the violin as I found out as I was leaving the ship, I could hear the strains of a dirge coming from his cabin.

When I say that life as a pilot in Guinea was different to that in Liverpool, I mean very different. Your responsibilities not only included as to when the ship could sail and to what draught it could load, but also to supervising the sailing of the pilot launch and making sure the crew turned up on time. This required the need to attend the jetty much earlier than normal to see if the crew were there. If not, it meant a hasty retreat to the village some two miles away to find them and drive them back to the jetty to make ready the launch. A task that was more onerous in the hours of darkness as there was no lighting and everywhere was pitch black. Time was of the essence as a lot of these bulkers did not like to come to the boarding point some 13 miles out to sea and sometimes, we would have to proceed out further before I could climb up the rope ladder suspended some 10 metres in length

Kamsar Port: Dave Devey climbing up a rope ladder to board a ship.

over the ship's side and make my way up 6 stairways to the bridge where I could meet the master. He would invariably be relieved to see me and hand over the navigation of his vessel to my care. In the two years I spent in Guinea I did not let any of them down and their ships came and went without serious mishap. That's not to say that accidents didn't happen, as witnessed when I was leaving the jetty on a refrigerated cargo vessel which had discharged its foodstuffs bound for the American style commissary. These frigo vessels visited once a month and brought much needed supplies of all manner of things including beer, breakfast cereals, baby food, and endless cases of Sprite for the children. On this occasion the vessel was berthed heading out to sea and the tide was ebbing fast at about 4 knots. The problem I was facing was of the stern rope catching in the propeller, which was showing half its blades out of the water as the vessel was only half loaded. I briefed the master of this problem and told him that the stern line would be the last rope to let go and that the officer based aft should inform the bridge when the rope was clear of the water. The "rope is now clear" signal duly arrived, and I ordered the engines "ahead". We cleared the berth and proceeded down the channel and on our way to sea. Then we received the bad news… From the poop deck came the message that the stern rope had disappeared over the side as it had got caught in the propeller. About halfway out we received a phone call from the engine room that there was a vibrating sound coming from the propeller shaft and it was overheating badly. A request was made by the Chief Engineer to stop the engines, but I told him this was not possible as we were passing through a shallow patch at the time with banks of mud on either side. We reduced speed to dead slow which seemed to have the effect of cooling the prop shaft and we were able to continue the passage till clear of the shoal patches. It was of course necessary to inspect the prop for any signs of damage, so the decision was taken to drop the anchor. By this time the pilot launch had arrived, so I descended the rope ladder and joined the crew of two to examine the evidence. The shaft was under water and was not visible due to the high sediment content of the muddy water but all of a sudden, a tail of rope surfaced some 10 yards from the stern. Yes, it was a piece of the stern rope and it was still attached to the ship. The Guinean crew set to work and dived into the water in turns each time chopping off large sections of the rope. This was an extremely brave thing to do as the presence of sharks presented a real danger. With instructions to the engine room to crank the shaft slowly in reverse and by hand the rope very slowly began to emerge from the deep, but progress was slow and it was getting near to sunset when everything would be pitch black and further work impossible. But undaunted, the two Guineans kept taking turns to dive down through the murky waters to the shaft with a kitchen knife borrowed from the ship lodged in their teeth and somehow managing to hack chunks of rope clear of the propeller. After three hours of continuous diving the final piece of rope surfaced, and the ship was free of the obstruction. I hailed up to the master that all was now clear and to show his gratitude he sent down two cartons of cigarettes and a case of bottled beer, and with the sun now gone and darkness having set in, we proceeded back to base in Kamsar. When I look back on this event, I can't help but think what would have been the consequences for that vessel if those Guineans hadn't volunteered to free that rope. The vessel would have been incapacitated until help came, and who knows how long that might have taken or where it would come from. The time lost, which is crucial to the running of a ship, would be very costly to the owners of the vessel. A sequel to this story was that on our hour-long return journey on the launch when everything was pitch black except for the tiny flicker of lights from the channel buoys, I took a bottle of beer from the case and asked the coxswain if he had a bottle opener. He looked at me in amazement and shook his head pointing to the AB (able seaman). I wondered what he meant but soon found out as the AB took the bottle from me and opened it with his shiny white teeth. I was still learning the ways of life in Africa! The crew later told me that they would rib this guy and say that he must be swallowing a little bit of beer each time he did this which was against his Muslim beliefs. But after this show of bravery, I developed a healthy respect for the Guinean crew members whose only reward was a few cigarettes and a case of beer.

I could write another book about my experiences whilst in The People's Democratic Republic of Guinea to give it its full title, as the two years I spent there were a life changing experience for me: of how my wife Pat gave birth to my lovely daughter Helene in the makeshift Guinean hospital, and who is now herself married with a daughter of her own; of how my two sons each contracted the Guinean worm which burrows sub-cutaneously and proved difficult to remove; of how I became very ill prior to leaving and finished up in The School Of Tropical Medicine Hospital back home in Liverpool; and of how my relief pilot colleague Peter Dawson was tragically killed in a road accident one month after he started piloting. But my abiding memories of this country are of the Guinean people themselves and their stoic acceptance of their situation where the life expectancy is about 35 years of age largely due to the ever-present malaria and the other tropical diseases that abound. I found them to be very friendly and interested to learn about life in Europe. It was a time when they were developing as a nation and I've no doubt they will be very much further down that road after I left in 1980. For myself, I became a stronger person from the experience with a much wider understanding of the pilotage world that is not exclusive to just Liverpool.

Pilots left to right: Dave Devey, Ibrahim Toure, & Terry Crowe.

CHAPTER NINE: RETURN TO LIVERPOOL

Our 2 years in the Republic of Guinea had come to an end, but not all was well – the boys had become infected by the Guinean worm, and I myself was feeling under the weather, although I did not yet know what it was.

This particular worm lies dormant in the ground until the rainy season arrives and then they start to hatch, at which time they go seeking a suitable host. The house we were living in Kamsar at that time had a sand covered garden instead of the usual grass, which was to stop snakes from entering - the most poisonous being the black mamba. Unfortunately, this was also an ideal environment for the Guinean worm in which to flourish. Kids like to play in sand. Guinean worms like kids who play in the sand. Bingo! Fortunately, these worms are harmless, but of course need removing, which presents a problem if you do not have the antidote to hand. If you try to remove them surgically (because they are very visible just under the skin) there is a danger of them leaving a part behind as they are removed, and that part will quickly grow again into a complete worm. We had tried treatment for the boys, but it had been unsuccessful, so my wife and I decided that we would seek treatment outside of Guinea now that the 2-year work contract was completed.

We packed our bags, said our goodbyes to everyone, and boarded the twin otter which took us to the capital Conakry, where we were scheduled to fly to Dakar in neighbouring Senegal. The reason for this trip was to register baby Helene with the British Consulate and obtain a British passport for her,

Family ready to board the twin otter to Conakry.

as we had already planned a trip to America before returning to the UK. I was in no fit state to do anything as I was only able to sip water, but we decided to continue anyway. We visited my cousin Irene in New York who sent me straight away to see a doctor who gave me some medicine to relieve my symptoms but needed more time to make a proper diagnosis. We were leaving the next day for Canada where we would meet up with our French-Canadian friends - the Fillion family who we met out in Kamsar. Etienne, known to us as Steve, worked out in Africa as an electrical engineer living with his wife Rosanne and daughter Suzanne. We became good friends and would meet at weekends if we were both free from duty. They lived in Quebec which was our next stop on our return journey home. These plans were made quite a while before I became ill, and we were unable to change them at short notice. We stayed with the Fillions for 3 days during which time I became progressively worse and could not wait to board the flight which would take us back to the UK where I could seek treatment for my increasing health problem. Pat was totally preoccupied with looking after the baby and was unable to be of help, and to compound the problem the estate agent who had rented out our house had forgotten to inform the tenants, so our house was unavailable for occupation. We were offered a temporary dwelling in a town called Upton which we accepted and moved in together with the boys, who both still needed treatment for their Guinean worms. I was now very weak and passing blood in a jelly-like stool and I asked my wife to ring for an ambulance which she duly did, and I was whisked off to Aintree and Fazackerley Hospital in Liverpool where the School Of Tropical Medicine had a special isolation ward. That is when my fortunes changed for the better. Following the routine tests for tropical illnesses I was diagnosed with amoebic dysentery and told that they had the necessary drugs to combat this, and I could expect a complete recovery. I cannot tell you how relieved I was to hear that as I thought my last days had arrived. Further good news came when Andrew and James were told that medicine was also available to kill the Guinean worms without the need for surgery, so that was also a great relief.

I spent 10 days in the hospital and gradually recovered my strength and was able to return to my old job as a Liverpool Pilot. Before I was permitted to act as pilot, I was obliged to accompany a number of other first class pilots on a familiarisation course to reacquaint me with the current changes during these last two years. Having completed the requisite number of trips, my licence to pilot was returned to me. There were one or two dissenters among my colleagues who felt that those of us who had left should forfeit their right to return, but in the main, the majority accepted us back and I soon slotted back into the old routine. We also got our own house back in Heswall after a month spent in a rental house and were able to start picking up the threads again of life in the UK.

My first reaction when back on the river was one of shock. In those two years spent away in Kamsar the traffic using the Port had changed dramatically. A lot of the regular visitors had disappeared off the scene, most of them never to return. The majority of them were the British companies like Cunard, Blue Funnel, Clan Line, PSNC, and Harrison Line among others who had previously carried their own appropriated pilots. The pilots who had left to go on secondment started to filter back from their various ports, mostly in the Middle East where they had handled the VLCCs (Very Large Crude Carriers) in places such as Jedda and Abu Dhabi. The secondment scheme was extended for a further period and more pilots took up the offer due to the continuing decline in traffic to the port.

This state of affairs continued to drag on for a number of years with pilots taking second jobs to supplement their reduced earnings. Eventually, the government decided that a new Pilotage Act was necessary, coupled with an offer of a lump sum payment to those pilots aged 55 and over who wished to take early retirement. The clouds were beginning to gather for the future of the Liverpool Pilotage Service which was in its 221st year of existence. A list was drawn up of those who wished to take up the offer and the 1987 Pilotage Act was born. The legislation was rushed through on what was termed a guillotine vote by the Thatcher government, with little time for parliament to debate the contents, the reason being that parliament was about to go into recess for the holidays. Harold Wilson, the former Labour prime minister - and now Lord Wilson Of Rievaulx and sitting in the House Of Lords, commented on the bill's implementation at the time by stating it was "An ill-conceived and hastily enacted piece of legislation". How right he proved to be. Certain key clauses in the act were ambiguous and could be interpreted differently depending on which side you were representing. The most ambiguous of them all was Clause 4 which contained the future status of pilots with relation to the newly created 'Competent Harbour Authorities' (CHA). Pilots viewed clause 4 as giving them the right to remain self-employed as prior to this act, the majority were. Some harbour authorities viewed it as the right to employ pilots and therefore gain control of this body of independent professional men. In addition to having control of the pilots, in Liverpool's case it would be for the very first time in their existence, the Pilotage Act would also give the CHAs control of the revenue earned from pilotage. Prior to the Act the revenue from pilotage, which was entirely separate from any other charges the harbour authorities made, was split 50/50 between the pilots and the authority. The pilot's half of the revenue would go towards the administration of the pilotage department, and the remainder as payment to each pilot depending on the class of licence he held. The Mersey Docks And Harbour Company (MDHC) as the designated harbour authority for Liverpool had long since sought control over the pilots and viewed their independent position with a great degree of jealousy. They saw the Act as an opportunity to take control of both the pilots themselves and the revenue they were earning. The pilots were shortly to find out how deep that jealousy ran.

At a general meeting of all pilots. barring those who were required for duty, held at Kingston House in Liverpool which was being used as a hostel for seafarers, the representatives announced that the only way that they could reduce the number of pilots in order to arrive at an acceptable working figure for future requirements would be to accept employed status under the CHA (Competent Harbour Authority). The members were informed that there was no alternative. The die was now cast.

The act contained a clause whereby pilots from ports which were overmanned could apply for interview to those ports which were short of manpower. With the bulk of trade now being with the European Common Market following our move to join being eventually accepted by France's President De Gaulle in 1970, the ports on the east and south coast began to increase their share of traffic at the expense of ports on the west coast such as Liverpool and Glasgow. A decision was taken at Liverpool that the junior pilots would be the ones who would need to seek a post elsewhere, along with all the time served apprentices who were not yet licenced, but the offer was open to any pilot however senior to also apply. I felt very sorry for the plight of the apprentices who had spent many years training, some as much as 7 years and working round the clock for very poor wages as employees of the Mersey Docks And Harbour Company, all in the belief that one day they would gain that coveted prize of a Liverpool Pilot's Licence. It was every apprentice's ambition, and under normal conditions the time span from joining the Service as junior lad and then progressing through the ranks to becoming senior lad was in the region of six years. It must have been a distressing time for them to have their dreams shattered and broken with little to show by way of qualifications when looking for another source of income. Many had no option but to return to sea and pick up where they had left off and train through the ranks and ultimately achieve a master's foreign-going certificate of competence.

The ports offering interviews to fully licenced pilots were Hull, Middlesborough and Southampton, the vast majority being from Hull. Pilots over the age of 55 took their severance sum and disappeared off into retirement, leaving the remainder wondering what lay in store for them.

CHAPTER TEN: LIFE AS AN EMPLOYEE

September 1st, 1988 will be a date etched on every serving Liverpool Pilot's memory. It was the day when our new employer took over the reins of management, and those of us who remained presented themselves for duty. We were about to experience life in the employment of a company following 222 years of independence. New representatives were elected to replace the ones who had left on early retirement. At the request of the new port management, they set out to devise a system of working that would attempt to replicate the one which we had used when we were self–employed. The salary level proposed by The MDHC came as little surprise to us and put us at the bottom of the scale when compared with other UK pilots. This was the start of many disputes which subsequently ensued as employees of a company who were hell bent on subduing us as a body of men. The representatives took our case to arbitration which resulted in a modest increase which even then, was well below the earnings of the other UK ports. In particular, it was well below the level of earnings agreed for Southampton Pilots, with one of their members sitting on the arbitration panel and endorsing the lower level for Liverpool. A factor that had an influence on the committee's verdict was that it came to light that the payment of additional fees to those pilots who had been appointed to shipping companies was still in existence. Prior to the meeting, the CHA had agreed with the representatives that these payments would be excluded from the proceedings, but subsequently reneged on the arrangements and raised this practice at the tribunal as being part of a pilot's earnings. Yes, appropriation had been allowed to continue and the problem once more reared its ugly head, but this time doubly so. Under the old system appropriated pilots' earnings were not disclosed and hence, a figure could only be guessed at, but now individual payments were being made each time a ship was manoeuvred, and everyone was aware of the amount paid out.

Again, there were no invitations being published offering pilots to apply for an interview, but the appointees name would be announced shortly after the post had been filled. This now created a situation of 'haves' and 'have nots', with a considerable disparity in the earnings between the two factions, which led to a return to that discontent which had plagued the Service whilst in self-employment. Coupled with the low salary and little prospects of joining the private band of the elite, some pilots decided to look elsewhere for employment and I became one of them. The Port of Southampton was seeking to recruit new pilots and I applied for an interview along with a number of others from Liverpool. I was pleasantly surprised to receive an invitation to attend an interview and duly headed south for the appointed day. It was a totally different world to that of Liverpool and I was stunned at the beauty of the Solent and its surrounding environment.

Southampton and the Solent.

I could immediately see what a wonderful life it must be as a Southampton Pilot, and in addition the salary was considerably higher than that in Liverpool. I returned home following my interview and eagerly awaited the mail in the days following. The envelope duly arrived and dropped through the letter box. I had mixed feelings about what the contents of it might contain which ranged from "I didn't do too badly at the interview, but maybe I wasn't posh enough to be accepted coming from Scouseland." So it was with bated breath that I gingerly opened the envelope and started to read the contents. Wow! I had been successful at the interview and was being offered a position as a trainee pilot in the Port Of Southampton. I was overjoyed at the news even though I was 47 years old and starting again at the bottom rung of the ladder. I showed the letter to my wife who made no comment at the time, so I took it as her usual indifference to matters concerning my work and I started to prepare mentally for the new chapter in my life. It would involve my studying of the Southampton Pilotage district with its tidal quirks and navigable channels including all the buoys and their distinctive identifying lights. I went to the next meeting of Liverpool Pilots and expressed my opposition to the reimplementation of the appropriation system and commented that I had been to Southampton for an interview, and whilst standing on the platform at Havant Railway station a thought struck me "Here am I a 'haven't' in Havant." This drew a howl of laughter from a somewhat previously sombre audience, but I felt I had made my point.

My feeling of elation at being selected for a post at Southampton was soon to be deflated, however. My wife suddenly dropped the bombshell that she would not be accompanying me on my new venture but would remain on Merseyside. The reason given was that our youngest child Helene who was now 10 years old (born in the Republic Of Guinea in 1980) had just been awarded a place at Upton Convent School in The Wirral, and she felt the upheaval of moving would be too much for her. This was a blow to me as it would mean commuting to Southampton for each spell of duty and living in bachelor accommodation whilst there. I was beginning to cool on the idea of going south. Then I received a phone call which helped to swing my decision back to remaining in Liverpool. It came from my fellow pilot and lifetime friend Terry Crowe, who had worked with me during my last year in Port Kamsar in Guinea. He pleaded with me not to go to Southampton but to stay and fight for the future of the Liverpool Pilot Service, which was daily sinking further beneath the waves under the control of our new masters - The Mersey Docks & Harbour Company. I agonised over a few nights as to what I should do. To turn down the golden opportunity which presented itself with a move to a glamorous new job with better remuneration, against the alternative of a future having to live with a system of inequality with one's fellow men whilst still doing the same level of work. This created a huge dilemma for me as the decision would result in the turning point of my life. I received yet another phone call from the representatives asking me when I was going to Southampton to which I replied, "I'm not going, I've decided to stay!" I knew this news would not be welcome as I had developed a reputation amongst my colleagues as being somewhat of a troublemaker due to my opposition to the way in which we were heading steadily downhill in our dealings with the CHA. I wrote a letter to Southampton Port Authority thanking them for their kind offer of employment but explained my reasons for having to decline. For the second time in my career, I found myself making a decision which in effect burnt my boats with regards to employment outside of Liverpool. I resigned myself to what the future may have in store for me on my home patch, but little could I have imagined how it really did pan out.

CHAPTER ELEVEN:
THE BATTLE FOR FREEDOM

I suppose we should have known what the CHA had in mind for us judging by the living quarters that we were allocated. The building had previously been home to a group of tally men who used to work at the nearby Woodside landing stage counting the heads of live cattle shipped in from Ireland. The trade had fallen away to one ship per week, so the rooms became vacant, and we were handed the keys and duly moved in.

To say it was sparse would be a gross understatement. As you opened the paint-peeling green and brown front door, you were faced with the sight of an old-fashioned toilet complete with overhead cistern and rusting chain. The front door was also the door to the toilet, so if anybody was using it and somebody opened the front door from the outside, then the poor unfortunate incumbent would be caught "in flagrante delicto". The accommodation consisted of a small kitchen with a Belfast sink and two other rooms with an adjoining entrance. The first room was just big enough to fit two armchairs and a coffee table, and from it a staircase led to an upstairs sleeping area in which were situated two single beds. The staircase was bare and screened off from what would become the lounge by means of old piece of curtain. The bedroom area (if you could call it that) was unheated and without any washing facilities and everywhere was damp. The only source of heating was from two electric night storage heaters which consisted of house bricks situated inside a metal jacket, which were heated during the night when the price of electricity was cheaper, and during the daylight hours gave off what little heat that they had acquired the previous night. The ultimate farce was the provision of an electric heater in the lounge which only worked if a button was pressed, which was hidden behind one of the armchairs and would then give off heat for ten minutes whence it needed to be reprogrammed. In the winter months particularly, it was less than adequate and the only way to keep warm was to remain fully dressed. It is important to note that pilots work 24/7 and operate at all hours of the day and night dependant on the times of the tides and need somewhere where they can relax in some sort of comfort, whilst awaiting the phone call that will send them to join the launch waiting at the nearby Woodside landing stage.

Woodside Landing Stage.

It will then take them on a one-hour journey out into the open sea where they will then climb a rope ladder hung over the ship's side, ascend the numerous stairways leading to the ship's bridge, and meet the captain to explain to him exactly what they intend to do to bring the ship safely into port. Their job is only just starting. They are not there to advise, as government would have you believe, but are there to oversee and direct the complex and difficult operation, a plan of which they have already presented to the ship's master. I know that I have mentioned this before in a previous chapter, but this time round I thought it necessary to highlight the lack of support coming from the harbour authority to assist the pilots in the performance of their onerous duties. It was at the time a standing joke amongst the fifty pilots that remained in employment, that only one person had ever used the sleeping facilities because it was so damp. He described his experience as "Piling on the blankets and waiting till the steam started to rise before he would be warm enough to drop off to sleep". So that was our introduction to life in the employ of the newly created Competent Harbour Authority aka The Mersey Docks & Harbour Company. It did not serve to endear them to us, and sadly that sentiment would prevail throughout our unfortunate relationship. To further understand our position within the company's structure of management, we were presented with an organigram which showed the various levels at which the employees who were in the marine department were placed. It showed the pilots to be on a level with a dock master, whose job was to open and close the gates when a ship transited the locks from the river and into the docks. We posted this organigram on the notice board for all to see, which infuriated the body of pilots who now realised that their skills and expertise gained over many years of training, notwithstanding the daily hazards created by the unpredictable Irish Sea weather, were neither recognised nor appreciated by their new masters - The Mersey Docks & Harbour Company. A rift between the two parties began to open which would grow ever wider as the authority attempted to tighten its grip on their control over pilots. The Pilotage Act had already given them possession of the revenue from pilotage, which was a separate and distinct charge made to the ship owner for pilotage services rendered. The pilots' previously agreed share of 50 per cent when in self-employment now went straight into the coffers of the CHA, who were hell bent on squeezing even more of the revenue and pilots were seen as ready targets.

It was about this time that I became one of the four representatives who were elected by the body of the pilots to negotiate the terms and conditions of employment with the CHA. The system at that time was for just two of the representatives to attend the various meetings with the CHA personnel manager, and report back to the body of pilots at their monthly meetings held at Woodside. I was not one of the two negotiators and was informed of the outcome of the meetings sometime after the event. I was beginning to become frustrated and angry that we seemed to be losing more and more ground for very little or no return. As each month passed, and months ran into years, I became more and more unhappy to see what little that was left of the life that we had inherited being further slowly chipped away. The reason being given by the reps for our ever-declining situation which kept coming back following meetings with the MDHC was that "There is nothing we can do to stop them. They are now our employers, and they can now call the shots".

The room which served as a meeting place was far too small to accommodate the numbers who regularly attended the monthly meetings and some of our members had to remain in the lounge and strain to listen to what was being said. The meeting room consisted of a full-size billiard table set in the middle of the floor and long red leather benches on each side which had been rescued from our earlier residence and were somewhat the worse for wear. Along with some oil paintings of sailing pilot cutters, these items were all we had left to remind us of those halcyon days when we had our own pilot office on Canning River Wall from where the business of pilotage was conducted. It is still there to this day despite the MDHC telling us at the time that it was no longer safe, and we needed to evacuate the building. That was the same red brick building that I mentioned in a previous chapter when I was summoned to my interview at the tender age of 16 and only just into long trousers. Today it is part of the Maritime Museum and still standing safely! We were informed that suitable accommodation was available in their building at the Liverpool Pier head (one of the Three Graces). The "suitable" accommodation turned out to be in the basement of the building below ground level with no windows, whilst the senior managers of MDHC were ensconced on the top floor having sumptuously furnished rooms and a wonderful view of the River Mersey and the busy shipping movements. We pilots who actually operated on the river had no such view in fact no view at all. That should have told us where we stood within the company's structure of importance long before we ventured to become their employees. So, from being an independent group of professional men organising our own operations, we now became foremen in a company that was hell bent on destroying what little dignity there was left in our ranks. We were also divided amongst ourselves due to the iniquitous system of appropriation whereby junior pilots were out earning their more experienced elders, having been appointed by dubious methods which ranged from freemasonry to nepotism. The morale of the Service was very low and as each month went by, we found ourselves sinking lower and lower into the mire of despair, and dissatisfaction that being stripped of one's dignity brings.

Election time came round again for the position of representative, and of the four serving reps, mine was the only one to go forward, the other three deciding to resign their posts. Being the one and only representative putting his name forward I felt it my duty to seek some support. I picked up the phone and dialled the man who had previously rung me urging me not to go to Southampton but to stay and fight, Terry Crowe. I didn't need to remind him of our previous conversation as he too was aware of the gravity of the situation and knew the purpose of my phone call. He readily agreed to support me and put his name forward as well. It was to be the start of a partnership that would last to this day, as we look back on the chapter of events that took place over a period of seven years.

Dave Devey & Terry Crowe.

Two more reps were recruited, namely Bob Moses and Tony Booth, and we did not have long to wait before the first attack on the body of our men came. It came in the form of an advertisement in the local newspaper - The Liverpool Echo, for the post of "2 Pilots for the Port of Liverpool". The salary was a lot less than that agreed at arbitration and the proposed training scheme would only allow for a handful of pilots to achieve the position of First Class Pilot. Most of the would-be applicants would never reach that position. When challenged with this downgrading of the status of our future pilots the MDHC replied that decisions made at arbitration are not binding and that therefore they were legally entitled to do this. To a group of men who still harboured beliefs that the future of our existence lay within the next generation of pilots, what was being imposed upon us was totally unacceptable. In the previous self-employed training scheme, all pilots were obliged to reach the top level within a set period of time deemed to be safe, in order to gain as much experience as possible and as early as possible in the handling of the largest ships. The CHA's plan was to keep pilots at a lower level until invited to a higher class, thus saving money in salaries. This was totally contrary to our view that a pilot needed to gain that experience as early as it was safe to allow. A reduction in numbers was also on the CHA's agenda, with the intention of reducing the pilots from 50 to 43 in contravention of the arbitrations decision that 50 should be the proper number for Liverpool. All these changes were to be implemented without discussion or any input from the pilots themselves.

It was at this point that I proposed to the body of men that we needed to be much more closely associated with the local trade union which was the Transport & General Workers (T&G) based in Islington, Liverpool. If we intended to stand and fight against these intended changes to our lives, we needed the strength of the union to protect us from any retaliatory measures that the MDHC might decide to take against us, especially those who would be involved in any negotiations. The ensuing vote was in favour of doing this, so we discussed it with the local T&G and were officially sanctioned as full members. We were already allied to the T&G through membership of the United Kingdom Pilots Association, so it was done quite swiftly. Our monthly meetings were now held at Transport House in Liverpool and the representatives would be given the title of shop stewards. We were about to meet the opposition head on in a meeting arranged at their headquarters at the Liverpool Pier head. Their personnel manager Allan Price introduced himself and proposed that we address each other using first names. We were in no mood to cosy up to the very people who were attempting to suppress our future existence and replied that we would prefer to stay formal and use surnames prefixed by "Mr". None of our team including myself, had ever been to a meeting of this nature before, so we were adlibbing as we went along. Terry Crowe later described this in his book as "Tilting at windmills" a reference to the behaviour of Don Quixote, but we very soon picked up the negotiating posture, albeit a little unorthodox. We asked why the MDHC had decided to change the terms and conditions for new recruits from that agreed at arbitration. The reply came back that they had already stated that decisions made at arbitration were not binding and as employees of a company that we had no rights to oppose any actions that they chose to take. We reported back to the membership what had transpired, and their reaction was one of extreme anger that MDHC had chosen to take this route and that we needed to fight for the very future of our service. It was deemed unacceptable that future pilots should be paid any less than we were currently earning as we were already one of the lowest paid pilot services in the UK. Our colleagues in the Manchester Pilot Service were out-earning us and had earlier been approached by MDHC with a view to the two services amalgamating in order to further reduce costs. Manchester pilots had chosen to remain in self-employment after the inception of the 1987 Pilotage Act and not surprisingly declined the MDHC's invitation. The treatment that had been meted out to Liverpool Pilots had not gone unnoticed by their counterparts in Manchester and the poor level of pay in Liverpool gave them little incentive to wish to join such a scheme. The whole plan collapsed and in hindsight, Manchester must have been thankful to have made that decision.

So, the fightback began in the defence of the future trainees. It was now December 1991 and we had been in the bondage of the Mersey Docks & Harbour Company since that fateful day in October 1988 when we surrendered our freedom. The four representatives called for regular meetings with MDHC, but each time we met we were rebuffed and told that the plan to reduce the earnings of new pilots would go ahead. One of their tactics in meetings was to divert attention away from the important issues by switching the dialogue from one rep to the other, thus breaking the main theme of our argument. It was after one of these fruitless meetings that I told the other reps that we could not continue in this manner and that in future there would only be one speaker, and that was me. If any of them were unhappy with what was being said, then they were free to call a recess and we would retire to a back room to discuss the problem. Fortunately, they all agreed to this plan as I was not prepared to continue as before. Following any meetings, the four reps would all repair back to the billiard table at our Woodside HQ and discuss amongst ourselves just what had been said. These wash up meetings proved to be very important in being able to assess just what exactly the MDHC had in mind for us in the future. At this point we approached the T&G union and asked them what we could do to prevent the CHA from going ahead with their scheme. They explained the various alternative actions that we might wish to take in keeping within the bounds of the law at that time (it's now very much different).

The CHA had already started to interview the new applicants so it proved that they were hell bent on forcing through their changes, so action needed to be taken if we intended to combat the situation, and soon. It took the form of a ballot for industrial action which would include a withdrawal of our labour i.e., a strike. The members voted overwhelmingly in favour of such action and the MDHC were duly informed of the date it would start and the period of time for which it would last. History was being made. Liverpool Pilots had never been on strike before in the whole history of the Service, but we felt fully justified in our reasons for taking such drastic action. The harbour authority responded by refusing to attend any further meetings until we dropped the intended strike action. On the afternoon prior to the strike which was due to start at midnight, the CHA called for a meeting the following day and to postpone the strike whilst talks went on. This we agreed to do, and we put the action on hold. In the ensuing discussions they agreed to maintain the level of salary for the new recruits and a training programme suitable to all parties was agreed and the strike action was called off.

A period of semi peace ensued during the next few years, and we turned our attentions to renovating our living quarters at Woodside. A small group of some six pilots which included myself and Terry Crowe set about rebuilding the interior of the property. The first items to go were the brick-filled night storage heaters care of a sledgehammer. Not before we had contacted British Gas to connect us up to their system, as the building was without this facility. Once connected to the gas we booked a firm to come and install central heating throughout the building, which included the bedroom area, thus negating the need to raise steam using blankets in order to generate enough heat for sleep. Carpets with underlay replaced Marley tiles on the floors, and the lounge fireplace was cleared of discarded house bricks which filled the chimney area right up to the bedroom. A bathroom and shower cubical were installed upstairs, and the moth-eaten billiard table given a new green beige, and the benches were sent away to be reupholstered in red leather. All these jobs were completed either by professionals or our own labour over a period of years and the bills sent to the Harbour Company care of the new Pilot Manager, an Australian by the name of

Steve Knuckey. He had succeeded to the post following the retirement of our previous senior rep Bob Glover who had occupied the post since 1988 on the day of the changeover. The Marine Operations Manager John Whiteside was sympathetic to our situation, and because we were doing most of the labour ourselves, he sanctioned the payments. He was duly rewarded for his cooperation in the refurbishing of our accommodation when on his retirement the pilots presented him with a crystal Tantalus and six cut glasses. He was quoted later as saying that the pilots had given him a bigger send off than the one he had received from the MDHC.

The peace however was not to last and in the annual pay talks which always finished with us being given a less than inflation increase, the personnel manager announced that the company had decided that we only needed 43 pilots for the port operation instead of the present number of 48. We pointed out that the arbitration award had set the figure at 50 pilots based on the annual total number of services being 7000 making 140 services per pilot per annum. It was almost three years to the day from our first brush with the authority and threat of strike action when this latest bombshell was to hit us. It was done in the usual manner of a 'fait accompli' directive without any recourse to dialogue. As you might imagine, the body of pilots were less than pleased with this edict and in particular, in the manner in which it was declared. Following further meetings with the MDHC called by ourselves and attended by our district union representative, their attitude was one of intransigence and a refusal to move from their entrenched position. To avoid the proposed action being implemented, the pilots voted for industrial action for the second time in their lives. This time the battle became extremely tense with threats made that things would not be the same should we proceed with our intentions to withdraw our services. A plan was hatched by the authority to allow the ship's master of a large oil tanker to negotiate a passage through the main channel to the berth at Tranmere Oil Jetty without a pilot being present. This was considered by our side as being an extremely dangerous and irresponsible act, should they allow this act to take place. Our response was to contact the towage crews who might be asked to assist in this proposed venture, who agreed not to take part on the grounds of health and safety. The boatmen who are responsible for taking the heavy steel wires from the vessel and landing them ashore were also not prepared to participate in this action, again on the grounds of the dangers involved when local knowledge of working procedures was absent. The very fact that a responsible harbour authority would even contemplate such an action with all the dangers involved including pollution and even loss of life gives a good indication of their idea of what constitutes a safe procedure. Things were now getting very serious as we had now arrived at the last day of notice to strike, and the MDHC were adamant that they would not back down. The strike was due to start at midnight that night and a special meeting of pilots had been called for 2200 hours at Woodside. The MDHC called for an eleventh-hour meeting at their HQ and this time the Port Operations Director Bernard Cliff was in attendance. At last we were in the presence of the person who was briefing the personnel manager Allan Price as to company policy with reference to pilotage. It was an opportunity for us to express our grievances to the top man and to make him aware of how we felt. The meeting commenced at 2000 hours and proved to be a stormy one. Accusations as to who was responsible for the present situation were levelled from both sides with little in the way of agreement. A crucial point in the agenda was when Bernard Cliff's secretary slipped into the room and whispered something in his ear that made him turn very angry. He asked to know how the press had become informed of our intended action as we were subject to the company's gagging order about divulging company business to outsiders. Breaking with our agreement to not speak, one of our reps leaped to his feet and said "I hope you are not implying that a Liverpool Pilot would do such a dastardly thing", which seemed to placate him somewhat. Thank God he said it, as it spared my blushes and having to personally deny any involvement in the matter. We knew that it was crucial to our survival to tip off the press as to what was happening. This seemed to tip the scales in our favour, and after much heated discussion a compromise was reached in that the MDHC agreed to recruit two new pilots to bring our numbers to 50 again as per the arbitration findings, with a promise of further discussions on our pay claims. We were able to get back to Woodside just in time for the meeting and after relating the events of the earlier meeting, a vote was taken as to whether to suspend the strike until the outcome of the pay negotiations was known. The vote was in favour so again, we had come within minutes of strike action and had once more pulled back to allow the CHA to join us round a table and discuss the issues that were causing us major concern.

The year was 1995 and we had been in employment for 7 years and had spent a lot of the time defending the award given at arbitration from the attacks of the MDHC. But events were to take a major turn in the autumn of that year. The Port Managing Director Bernard Cliff was involved in a serious road accident whilst driving to catch a train to the company hostel in London and died two days later from his injuries. It would be a year later that the MDHC made their next attack on the pilots which would result in our third ballot for industrial action. It concerned our pilot station based near Amlwch (pronounced Amlok) on the northeast coast of Anglesey. This custom-built accommodation being close to Point Lynas lighthouse was constructed in the days when we were self-employed and replaced the cruising pilot boats mentioned in an earlier chapter. The architect, Joy Hockey was the wife of one of the serving pilots Phil Hockey. It was built using local stone and blended in

Point Lynas Pilot Station, Anglesey.

perfectly with the surrounding environment of a rock-strewn headland with patches of grass which led down to a boarding jetty in Eilian Bay. The ground floor contained a kitchen and spacious dining room which adjoined the bedroom area of eight separate rooms and an ensuite bathroom. Upstairs was a large lounge area with views out to the west where approaching vessels could be monitored and tracked (a bit different to the view we had in the Dock Company basement mentioned earlier). The lounge ceiling was in a V shape and was clad entirely in pine which had been varnished to a high gloss. It was situated in the ideal spot for boarding ships approaching from the west as the prevailing wind was westerly and frequently blew hard. The shelter of the land in Elain Bay where the jetty was situated gave ideal conditions for boarding ships even in gale force winds, which made the Lynas station the principle boarding station. Pilots would arrive by taxi which was a two-hour journey from Woodside, and then find a bedroom to sleep in before their ship was due to arrive. The lighthouse was manned by pilots whose job was to direct the ships to a safe boarding area when embarking their pilot. Each bedroom was connected to the lighthouse by telephone and the pilot would be alerted in time to board his ship. The jetty was a two-minute walk from the dormitory and a fast launch would be waiting to take him to the boarding position.

So, there would be a constant flow of pilots either inward bound or outward bound and those on the station at mealtimes would have food prepared for them by a team of local ladies who attended on a daily basis.

So, when the bombshell was dropped that the MDHC was in negotiations with the National Trust to sell this building to them for use as a ramblers hut, you can imagine what the pilots' reaction was. I can tell you we were outraged that they did this without any consultation or information as to what were their plans. Very soon we discovered that they planned to move us to a boarding house in the village of Amlwch itself, in the middle of a housing estate. We stated that this would be impractical as we come and go at all hours of the day and night which would create a noise nuisance to nearby neighbours. The plan unfolded further in that we were told that the launches would only operate from the Port of Amlwch situated some one and a half miles to the west of Eilean Bay and with no protection from westerly winds. The time had now arrived to hit back. It was us pilots who would have to endure these changes which were both impractical and dangerous. Again, faced with a situation which we could not afford to lose, we approached the union with our grievances. Further to this we contacted all the MP's (Members of Parliament) whose constituencies bordered on to the River Mersey and informed them of the situation. One of them was a former Liverpool Pilot Sir Malcolm Thornton, who had chosen not to be employed in 1988 and had left to go into politics becoming the MP for Crosby. We requested a meeting in the Houses of Parliament, and he duly arranged it. The T&G had approved our request for a ballot for industrial action and we made preparations to withdraw our labour for the third time. Our meeting with the MPs at Westminster gained us strong support for our cause and resulted in Malcolm Thornton obtaining a meeting with the chairman of the MDHC Trevor Furlong in order to state our objections to the proposed changes. The reasons given by the harbour authority for their actions was to reduce the costs of running the western station notwithstanding the fact that the bill for pilotage was paid by the ship owner and not the Mersey Docks And Harbour Company. Today, looking back on those three attacks from the harbour authority that were aimed specifically at pilots I realise now that it was an orchestrated attempt on their part to try to make us fit into their company structure as befits the rank of a foreman. The organigram that we were given depicting us at the level of foremen should have given us warning of what was to follow. Much lower pay for new recruits and only a handful to reach the top grade, poor living quarters, a reduction in numbers below the arbitration level, and finally stripping us of our hostel at Lynas and substituting it with a boarding house in the middle of a housing estate far distant from the boarding area which was open to the vagaries of the weather in the Irish Sea.

CHAPTER TWELVE: DELIVERENCE

A wind of change was blowing through the corridors of the Mersey Docks and Harbour Company, and it manifested itself in the form of a man called Peter Jones. Peter was the replacement Managing Director for the late Bernard Cliff. The ballot for industrial action was still in place and both parties had agreed to take the dispute to the office of arbitration situated in Garston, a suburb of South Liverpool. Peter Jones headed up their team along with Brian McShane - the Harbour Master, and Steve Knuckey - the Pilotage Manager, which was viewed as a welcome sign by the pilot representatives as we would be negotiating with the man who would be making the decisions on their side and not via the Employee Relations Manager. On our side was the district union officer Dave McCall, myself and the three reps. The meeting got underway and was heading in the usual direction of neither side being able to agree, when Peter Jones asked me what exactly was I looking for? I replied "Self employment would be our first choice, obviously." Then he came out with those words I shall never forget "Then why don't we talk about self-employment?" I could have fallen off my chair in astonishment… Here we have the principal officer of The Mersey Docks & Harbour Company inviting us to talk about a subject that was dearest to our hearts following eight years of abject misery as their employees. I recovered my power of speech as quickly as I was able and replied that we would be more than pleased to do that. At this point the union officer declared that discussions on the subject of self-employment were not in his remit, and he was obliged to withdraw from the meeting. The arbitration officials said that we could stay and continue our meeting using their premises even though it was no longer an arbitration matter. So it was left to the pilots and the MDHC to iron out their differences with Peter Jones as their spokesperson and myself speaking for the pilots. Peter outlined what would be their basis for any kind of a settlement and we were asked to produce figures identifying the annual costs which were incurred by the MDHC in the running of the pilotage operation, and how that would translate into a self-employed operation. He was anxious to see that there would not be any extra costs incurred by the MDHC. It was obvious from this moment on that an agreement could not be reached on that day and a different venue was arranged for the next day in the village of Daresbury, which was home to Lewis Carrol - the author of Alice In Wonderland. We were truly already in our own wonderland.

We had already done our homework and had followed each annual report issued by the MDHC showing the revenue earned from pilotage. This was a separate entry from all the other port charges as it was levied from the ship owner specifically for pilotage. This was how we were able to keep a track of how much the MDHC were pocketing from the charges for pilotage services and how little of it was being paid to the pilots. As I've mentioned before, we were traditionally awarded half of this amount when previously self-employed and the harbour authority kept the other half to pay for the cost of running the launches. So this figure was our target to achieve in the ensuing negotiations which ran on into a third day of discussions, this time at the Mollington Banastre Hotel close to the city of Chester. The talks ran on into the evening of the third day and the gap between the two sides was getting ever narrower. Could we do it? The principal difference in the new arrangement we were about to embark on from the one we were leaving was the percentage increase in the annual lump sum payment. We asked that our share of the annually declared revenue from pilotage be adjusted at the same percentage difference that the CHA published in their annual accounts. This was the comparison between the previous year's figure and the present years figure. I felt that this was the only way that we could claw back some of the monies that we had been denied whilst employees. Peter Jones asked me "What if the amount turns out to be less than that of the previous year? I said we would accept the loss of income but would adjust our numbers accordingly as and when pilots retired. Conversely, if the figures showed an increase in the previous year's revenue, then we would adjust our numbers upward to compensate. It would also save us many tedious hours of pay negotiations as the new annual figure would be just a simple equation. As a result, he agreed to accept this method of payment which would have a substantial impact on our future earnings in years to come. Our observations during our 9 years in their employ had shown that their annually published revenue of pilotage charges increased by an average of 6.7 per cent year on year, whilst we would be given one or two percent salary increases. Arriving at the final stages of our negotiations the two sides differed on three items involving charges for taxis, charges when a pilot is carried outside of the district when unable to disembark due to bad weather, and expenses whilst carried away. These points were acting as a stumbling block to a final agreement. It was about eight p.m. when Peter Jones asked for a recess and their team left the room to discuss the situation. When they came back some 15 minutes later Peter read out their decisions. He awarded us all three points, which to me was a magnanimous gesture as our target figure was now met and we could shake hands on the deal. I did hasten to mention that any implementation of the agreement would be subject to a vote of the pilots, and that was acknowledged. So on the evening of Saturday February 20th 1997, the seeds of a new self-employed pilotage service for Liverpool were sown. We could now return to Woodside to explain the proposed agreement to the pilots at a specially convened meeting the next day. On our way back home that evening Terry Crowe and myself stopped off at a pub called The Greenland Fisheries in the village of Neston in The Wirral. I was feeling very excited at the prospect of a return to the life we had all been used to and I drank my first pint for many months in celebration of our situation. There was however one caveat and that was "What happens if the pilots vote it down?" We would find the answer to that question following a ballot of all the members the next day. Our job now was to try to sell the idea to the men before such a ballot took place.

The meeting at Woodside lasted for most of that day with many members expressing their various concerns as to how it would all glue together. The greatest incentive to vote in favour was the increase in remuneration which would happen as a result. Terry used to quip to me "How do you catch a pilot fish?" Answer: "With a dollar bill on the end of a hook". The vote to explore the concept of a self-employed service went 36 for and 2 against with no abstentions.

We started our preparations for creating a service company by examining the working practices of three other self-employed pilotage services which included our neighbours Manchester Pilots Ltd, Tees Pilots, and Humber Pilots. Each of the three ports very kindly let us have a copy of their working rules covering all aspects of their pilotage operations. We were able to extract the parts that we liked from all three contracts and piece them together to form a suitable contract that would fit the bill for the pilotage operation in Liverpool. For example, we liked the Manchester idea of the formation of a cooperative with each pilot holding one share, and a limited-service company to enact the business of the cooperative. The Humber Pilots contract formed the backbone of our new contract for services, but there were certain clauses that we found to be unacceptable which we had deleted. Little did we know at that time that those very same clauses would be used against them by their CHA in a bid to take them into their employ. But more about that later. A constitution needed to be written governing the rules of the cooperative and the service company, and for this purpose we hired a local solicitor Richard Wilkinson to go over all the documents we had written and to ultimately produce a final draft, which was both informative and more importantly legally binding. The changeover to self-employment would include an offer for any pilot to join the Pilots National Pension Fund which was a final salary scheme specially created to cater for all UK pilots whether employed or self-employed. With the apprenticeship system now discontinued with the phasing out of the cruising pilot boats and their replacement with fast launches, the need for recruiting turned towards the pool of sea-going officers with experience as ship's master in command. Alternatively, authorised pilots from other UK ports would also be invited for interview. As part of the proposed new arrangements, we the pilots would be responsible for interviewing and enlisting new recruits to the service and training them for a six-month probationary period until they were suitably trained up to be examined for authorisation as a fourth class pilot. Thereafter, they would spend a further two years in each class of authorisation until fully qualified as first class. Each of these new responsibilities delegated to the Service Company had to be set out in the documents being prepared for the final day when the pilots would decide which road to take; either stay in employment or make the break and set out on a new and uncharted path down the road of self-employment. This would probably be the biggest decision any one of them would have to make and to this end I wrote a letter to every serving pilot urging them to take the latter route. Two further meetings were held with Peter Jones and a date of June 1st 1997 was decided on as the day when we would make the changeover. But first the pilots had to make their decision. A day was fixed when all pilots would individually attend at Woodside and read the 3 contract documents before making their final decision. Our secretary Andy Malcolm was present for the whole day to oversee the ballot procedure. The result of the vote was 46 in favour of self-employment with 2 in favour of remaining in employment. A similar number also voted in favour of a variable uplift in salary against a fixed amount decided annually by negotiation. We were nearly there.

The big day finally arrived, and we four representatives attended the signing ceremony along with Peter Jones and the MDHC team. A legally binding agreement was signed by all present giving the newly created Liverpool Pilot Service a contract for services with a five-year roll over agreed. We adjourned to the Crosby Hotel where Alan Price - the public relations manager joined us having said that he would like to have a drink with us. I found this gesture to be very gratifying when I considered the countless hours we had both spent in those previous 7 years arguing across the table over the many issues which had arisen. I was always aware that he was just doing his job and that the policies he was fronting were not of his making but were coming from higher up the chain. He was just the mouthpiece for the higher management of the MDHC. So now we were free at long last to once more have a say in all affairs to do with pilotage and to discuss any problems with the CHA as equals and not as subservient foremen. But a lot of work faced us in these early days to make sure that we kept our promise that we would offer a first-class service without confrontation, but with cooperation. What we didn't realise at that time was that there was another and much bigger threat to our newly found status about to rear its ugly head.

CHAPTER THIRTEEN: RETURN TO SELF-EMPLOYMENT

The responsibility for pilotage was once more in the hands of those who know and experience at first hand the vagaries of the daily life of the working pilot. Only a person who has experienced the act of boarding or disembarking from a ship using a rope ladder of 10 metres in length at night-time and in hazardous weather can know how dangerous this practice can be. It is a skill in itself, which if not quickly learnt by the newcomer to the profession, could have disastrous consequences when it comes to that moment of decision as to whether or not to make the jump between launch and ship. Management who live and work in a shore-based environment cannot possibly comprehend or appreciate just how difficult this task can be and it is something a pilot has to do every time he faces duty. Too many pilots worldwide have lost their lives, either through misjudgement, or have been the victim of a dangerously unsafe ladder. One of my good friends Bernard Trott, a Liverpool Pilot of vast experience, lost his life whilst disembarking from a vessel he had just piloted safely to an anchorage in the vicinity of the Mersey Bar Light Vessel. Whilst making the transfer from the ladder to the launch below which was pitching and tossing in the heavy seas, he lost his footing and fell into the water between the launch and the ship. The launch crew were unable to rescue him as there was a danger he could be crushed between the launch and the ship's side. The ship's master, on seeing the tragedy unfolding, rushed from the bridge and down to the main deck where he located a life belt and jumped into the

Liverpool Pilot Bernard Trott.

sea to assist Bernard who was by now feeling the effects of hypothermia and lapsing into unconsciousness. The captain got to him and brought him back to the pilot ladder where he attached a rope underneath his arms, and he was pulled up on board by the crew and laid on the deck where attempts were made to resuscitate him. Soon after, a rescue helicopter arrived and landed on the main deck where the medics attended to Bernard, and he was flown to hospital in Liverpool. Sadly, we learned later that he had died before he reached hospital. The sea in the winter months is very cold and estimates have been made that anyone falling in will only survive for about four minutes before succumbing to hypothermia and lapsing into unconsciousness. This is yet another example of why the profession should be given the respect that it deserves by harbour authorities and not treated as necessary evils. Praise should go to that very courageous captain in risking his own life by jumping into the sea in that weather, especially as it was just starting to go dark. To this day I don't know if he was ever given any credit for what he did, but I suspect not. Bernard and I had spoken the evening before about playing a game of golf when he got back. He would never see another golf course and left behind a widow and three children to mourn his tragic loss.

As the weeks passed, we settled into the new arrangement and felt that everything was going well with relations between the pilots and the harbour authority vastly improved. Then we received news of a serious threat to our new existence emanating from the government department DETR (Department of the Environment, Transport and the Regions) led by a civil servant by the name of Andrew Burr. Burr arrived on the scene having previously been involved in road planning (I believe it was the building of the Newbury bypass) and had no previous experience of port operations, and in particular pilotage. At that time, I was a member of the committee of the United Kingdom Maritime Pilots Association (UKMPA) based in London and my area of responsibility covered all ports in the northwest of England which included my own port Liverpool. London is where I was first introduced to Andrew Burr when he delivered a speech to the UKMPA. The delegates were pilots from all of the UK registered ports.

I listened intently to what he was saying and quickly picked up what his real intentions were regarding the future of the pilotage profession in the UK. Civil servants never actually say outright what they intend to do but talk a certain waffle that is only understood in government circles. Following hours of metaphors and phrases I was familiar with through my previous union meetings, he finally disclosed that he intended to visit a number of ports in the next few weeks to discuss a review of the 1987 Pilotage Act. It was clear to me that he was hell bent on a path which would lead to all pilots becoming employed by their respective CHAs. When I found out that Liverpool was not on his list of intended visits I wrote a letter to the Minister For Transport - Glenda Jackson (yes, the actress when she was a Labour Minister) asking that Liverpool be included in Andrew Burrs visits. She replied back that she would arrange for this to happen. I knew Andrew Burr did not want to come to Liverpool as he was aware of us having become self-employed, which was the exact opposite of what he was intending to do. I myself was alarmed that what we had fought for in those 9 years and were now just beginning to enjoy our newfound independence, would all be swept away by this new campaign. I met with Peter Jones who asked me if I wanted to hold this meeting with Andrew Burr as a joint venture, or would I prefer to meet him separately. I chose to meet him separately as I needed to have a long talk with Mr. Burr about what happened to us in 9 years of employment and how we were determined to keep what we had regained.

He arrived along with his assistants and took up his seat opposite to where I was sitting. I could see that he was less than pleased at having to come to Liverpool when it was not on his list of visits and he remained with folded arms throughout the two hours I spent telling him about our past experiences as employees of the Mersey Docks & Harbour Company; of our various strike actions, our poor remuneration, and our status within the Company's structure. One of the patterns of behaviour I learned to recognise when working at the union offices was that anybody who folds their arms when another person is speaking is indicative of the fact that that person is not listening to what's being said. When I had finished telling him that the 1987 Pilotage Act gave pilots the right to choose whether to be employed or self-employed under clause 4 (ii b), and that self-employment was the only solution to this problem, he had heard enough and made claim that he had a train to catch to his next appointment and hastily withdrew from the meeting. The battle to defend our new life had begun and we had fired the first shots.

I knew that he had no previous experience of maritime affairs, but I needed to know who was feeding him this information which was leading him down the path of support for all UK pilots to be taken into employment. The situation at that time was a fifty-fifty split, with half the pilots in the UK, employed and half self-employed. I eventually stumbled across the answer when I attended a meeting of UK Harbourmasters in London where I was representing the UK pilots. There I discovered Andrew Burr large as life and mixing it with the brethren on first name terms. I could see he was a familiar face in this community and knew his way around. He spotted me and carefully avoided any contact and not long afterwards he made his exit. So the pieces of the jigsaw were beginning to slot together. A number of the harbour masters were intent on taking control of pilotage for the power it gave them and control of the revenue associated with it, so here was the driving force behind Burr's agenda. It was to have grave consequences for the Humber Pilotage Service which at the time was the largest group of self-employed pilots in the UK, being 150 in number. A former Humber pilot and now a recently appointed harbourmaster - Paul Hames made a declaration to his erstwhile colleagues that he intended to take them into the employment of the harbour authority. Each pilot could apply for a job and the decision to employ or not would be decided by interview and Paul Hames himself would be the principal interviewer. There would be a substantial reduction in the numbers to be employed and a sharp cut in the pay structure. This declaration would lead to a pitched battle between the pilots and the CHA which would continue for many months. As a member of the committee of the UKMPA I was invited to attend their meetings in order to explain to them about our treatment in Liverpool at the hands of the CHA which resulted in nine years of conflict. I urged them to stick together and fight to maintain their status as self-employed professionals. Then I discovered that a small group of their members had already agreed to handle the large tankers that came to the port for an additional payment over and above the basic rate. This breakaway group would ultimately cause a rift in the membership which would get ever larger, and which would ultimately result in the demise of a long established and well-run pilotage service on the Humber River. I hear that its replacement service still has its problems to this present day with a high turnover of personnel who soon become disenchanted with the intensity of work and the low level of remuneration. A lot of the self-employed pilots could not bring themselves to participate in the new arrangement and either sought to return to a seafaring life or to take early retirement. They remain bitter to this day at the lack of support for their cause by the incumbent Labour Government, and in particular by John Prescott who was a merchant seaman before his elevation to the post of deputy prime minister. This lack of support for pilots by successive UK governments is at the root cause of the problems that beset the profession today. By contrast, their French counterparts are highly valued by their government and are the first to be consulted when problems arise within the port system. I was very disappointed to have lost that fight as I knew from personal experience what lay in store for those that signed up to it. Many years later I was invited to a meeting of the Humber Retired Pilots Society in company with Terry Crowe and we were suitably wined and dined and they presented me with a beautiful, framed picture of the "Commander Cawley" a Humber cruising pilot vessel depicted leaving Hull. Whilst I was very happy to be amongst people of my own persuasion who had somehow come to accept their fate and moved on to another way of life, I could not help but feel a great sadness that such a proud organisation with a long history of dedicated service to the Humber had ceased to exist

Commander Cawley.

and in particular, the manner in which it was assassinated. It served to mark one of the darkest days in the history of UK pilotage. Our old friend Andrew Burr played a leading role in supporting the Humber

CHA in this conflict which helped to bring about the demise of a once proud Pilot Service. The consequences of the disastrous fallout created by the sudden disappearance of 130 experienced pilots to be replaced by only 15 men who had opted to stay still has repercussions to this day. It brought about a distinct change of tack by Andrew Burr from his earlier campaign to push for all UK pilots to be employed, to one of a more conciliatory attitude of accepting the fact that self-employment would have to be tolerated. However, it did not stop him from inserting into the newly published Port Marine Safety Code that "employment was the default option" in the event that an agreement cannot be reached between the pilots and the CHA. The 1987 Pilotage Act which presently overrides this Code does not make any mention of this as it has been slipped into this document based solely on the opinion of the promulgater. Unfortunately, there are some people who believe that the Port Marine Safety Code supersedes the 1987 Pilotage Act and have acted accordingly. This is a dangerous misconception and could lead to CHAs attempting to take action against pilots without legal justification. Recent history has shown that a change to employment can sometimes lead to disastrous consequences for both the port and the pilots.

On a slightly brighter note, the pilots from the Port of Belfast asked me if I would go over to their headquarters in Northern Island to assist them in their ongoing dispute with the CHA. Belfast, like Liverpool, had opted to accept employment status in 1988 and afterwards, like Liverpool, had come to deeply regret having made the decision. They had heard about the happenings in Liverpool and wished to emulate that system and return to self-employment. The port management agreed to allow me to sit in on their meetings with the pilots and I was able to relate to them how things changed for the better in Liverpool after nine years of conflict. We had three separate meetings, each one of which ran for the whole day. An agreement was ultimately reached which gave back to the Belfast pilots their previous status as independent professional men contracted to the Port Authority. Tribute should be paid to the port management at Belfast who accepted to allow me to be present at the meetings and that further, they had listened without interruption to what I had to say. All this happened in 2005 and I still have contact with their senior representative Liam

MaGee who tells me that everything is running smoothly some 16 years later. They have chosen to mark the historic occasion with a plaque outside their headquarters in Belfast Port to commemorate their new way of life.

I was asked sometime later if I would be prepared to talk to the Clyde Pilots and explain to them the circumstances of the happenings in Liverpool, as they were in dispute with their CHA. I readily agreed and drove up to Glasgow along with Terry Crowe and met with Tommy Purse - their senior representative. I gave them a complete rundown of what had happened and advised them on the procedures they might wish to take to bring about a similar result in the Clyde pilotage district. I told them that whatever course they decided to take that they should all stick together and support each other to the conclusion of the dispute. I did not get any further follow up to my two meetings with them, so I gathered that they had decided against taking any sort of action.

Back in Liverpool it was election time for the position of representative and I put my name forward as normal but when the ballot result was announced I found I had been voted out of office.

The pilots favoured a younger candidate Chris Booker who was duly elected and Terry Crowe took the reins as Senior Representative which left me with the position of representative for the ports situated in the north west of the country as a sitting member of the section committee of the UKMPA based at Transport House in London. The UKMPA sheltered under the umbrella of the Transport & General Workers Union (T&G) and as such I represented Region 5 under the union-based structure. I have to admit that I was not a popular member of the committee as I found myself frequently in disagreement with the chairman's policies with regards to the defence or lack of defence of UK Pilots against attacks from government civil servants, Andrew Burr being the principal protagonist. Burr's primary role in the summary dismissal of 130 experienced Humber pilots to be substituted by a hastily recruited and ill-trained group of replacements was a wakeup call to those who had trusted him as a friend and ally of pilots. As a result of my objections to his stance, an attempt was made to get rid of me by altering the normal voting procedure and inviting two candidates to stand against me, one being a Harwich Pilot and the other a Tees Pilot. Neither of these candidates had a mandate to stand for election to Region 5 as they were both members of their own regions. Under the rules they could only be considered as a candidate for a region other than their own if there were no candidates' names put forward from that region. A protest was duly lodged by Liverpool Pilots indicating that this was a slight of hand and that the recognised voting procedure should be reinstated. This was met with fierce opposition from the chairman who accused me of being gutless for failing to stand against the two named persons. That struck a raw nerve with me, having recently led Liverpool in a nine-year war against the CHA. The real irony of it was that I had latterly helped his port of Belfast to obtain their freedom and now he was accusing me of having no guts! So the dispute went to the senior officers of the union who adjudicated on the matter and came down in our favour and normal voting procedures were reinstated. Subsequently I was re-elected for Region 5 and continued to defend the ports in my district for a further four years right up to the day of my retirement at the age of sixty-five. Within those four years I had an opportunity to meet up with Andrew Burr on his own territory at the DTLR (Department for Transport, Local Government and the Regions) in Westminster in company with the UKMPA chairman. The purpose of the meeting was to discuss and make comment on the latest draft of the Port Marine Safety Code which was intended to point the way to future safety practices for all UK port operatives which included pilotage. Andrew Burr was chairing the meeting and at one point I asked him if the Humber CHA was currently acting within the agreed recommendations of the code. He exploded with indignation and demanded to know who I was representing at this meeting. I was quite shocked at his aggressive manner and replied that I represented the ports in the northwest of the country. I knew that things were far from normal in Humberside following the dismissal of all of the pilots and that only 15 of the 130 had initially opted to take up the offer of employment. He never did give an answer to my question and I was never again invited to any of his meetings.

When I first joined the section committee of the UKMPA the logo emblazoned across the badge of the organisation read "United We Stand, Divided We Fall". To my shock and disbelief, a decision was taken to have these words removed from the official title of the UKMPA as no longer being necessary. I held the exact opposite view that these words were of paramount importance in our fight to maintain our independent status which was part and parcel of self-employment. UK pilots were already split down the middle with the implementation of the 1987 Pilotage Act which created two separate and distinct factions in the pilotage world: the one of independent professionals operating their own Service and the other of employees of the Harbour Authorities with little or no input into decisions involving their own wellbeing. The two different statuses are inextricably linked to the kind of remuneration that a pilot can expect to receive for the responsibilities and risks that are part and parcel of his profession. Needless to say, the self-employed pilots far outstripped their employed colleagues in both earnings and status.

My time as a working pilot was coming to a close, but not before one last and final venture that I got myself involved with in company with Terry Crowe. One of the areas that needed addressing was simulation training for pilots. We had visited some of the UK based units but found that they were unsuitable for pilot training as they did not cover the crucial area abaft of the ship's beam and therefore not possible to track other vessels which might be wishing to overtake. It was about this time that Liverpool's John Moores University had commenced building a unit near to the Cammell Laird shipyard, and Terry and I were invited to view the construction. They were about halfway into the build and we observed that it was going to operate within an arc of 220 degrees from right ahead. We quickly pointed out that we would not be using it to train our pilots which caused them to be quite concerned. We explained to them our reasons why it would not be suitable for our purposes, so they agreed to join us in a trip to Rotterdam to compare their simulation procedures with those operating in the UK. The setup in Rotterdam was very impressive and featured something we hadn't seen before, namely towage assistance with the use of tugs. We all came back to Liverpool with a totally different view of what was required for a successful operation for the training of pilots. An all-round panorama showing other traffic movements in conjunction with a separate unit operated and manned by experienced tug crew personnel was necessary in order to make the simulation as close to reality as possible. The problem was that John Moores had already built the main bridge structure, which only operated within 260 degrees and didn't allow for a view behind. They quickly modified their original plan and built an additional structure, supported by four legs which solved the visibility problem, and a room was fitted out with a towage unit.

Liverpool Pilots' Simulation Centre.

The finished product resulted in the UK's first all-round simulation centre which was ideal for the training of pilots and became the first choice for a number of UK based pilotage operations, which included both Southampton and Liverpool. However, this new technology needed to be treated with a degree of caution. On our visits to the different simulation centres in operation Terry Crowe and myself witnessed 'experts' demonstrating how to manoeuvre a large vessel and to guiding it into its berth. When we questioned these operatives as to their ship-borne experience and qualifications, they professed that they had never been to sea and therefore held no marine qualifications. We could see from the manner in which the models were being handled that they could not have been qualified pilots, which raised the question as to who should be teaching the rudiments of maritime simulation. Simulation should be seen as an aid to pilot training and not as a means of training. Sadly, some ports are abusing the system and are simulation training their new pilots without the need for tripping (accompanying an authorised pilot on board ship). Legislation needs to be brought in to stop the current malpractices which occur at some of these navigation schools whereby unqualified personnel are teaching ship handling and pilotage and issuing dubious certificates of competency. In the wrong hands, the simulator can quickly turn into a play-thing used like a toy and not replicating real life situations.

My career as a working pilot was drawing to a close and I wasn't unduly sad as I was beginning to find the pace of the job a little on the strenuous side. Pitching and tossing in a launch for over an hour, then climbing those rope ladders and negotiating the numerous stairways leading up to the bridge became more of a strain, then spending most of the night without rest and having to keep focused at all times until the vessel under my charge had safely traversed the pilotage district and was no longer my responsibility. After that came the task of retrieving the car which depended on which part of the dock estate that you had earlier left it parked. The luxury of every night in bed beckoned and it was hard not to be looking forward to the day when it would become a reality.

CHAPTER FOURTEEN: RETIREMENT AND VINDICATION

The first of the official farewells came by way of an invitation to attend Neston Cricket Club on December 20th 2006 where a gathering of well-wishers were assembled which comprised of Liverpool pilots both active and retired, and pilots from Belfast, the Humber and the Clyde. It came as a very pleasant surprise to see so many familiar faces that I had come to know in my career as a pilot and a member of the section committee of the UKMPA and it gave me a great feeling of camaraderie knowing that each one had experienced the same challenges and met with the same difficulties that I had in my forty years as a pilot. I was presented with a beautifully framed admiralty chart of the Liverpool pilotage district which stretches as far north as Saint Bees Head in Cumberland and south to the island of Anglesey. Anybody who wished to post a message on it alongside their signature was invited to do so. The resulting picture hangs in pride of place on the wall in my retirement bungalow in North Wales and serves as a permanent reminder of my erstwhile colleagues and friends whose memories I value highly to this day.

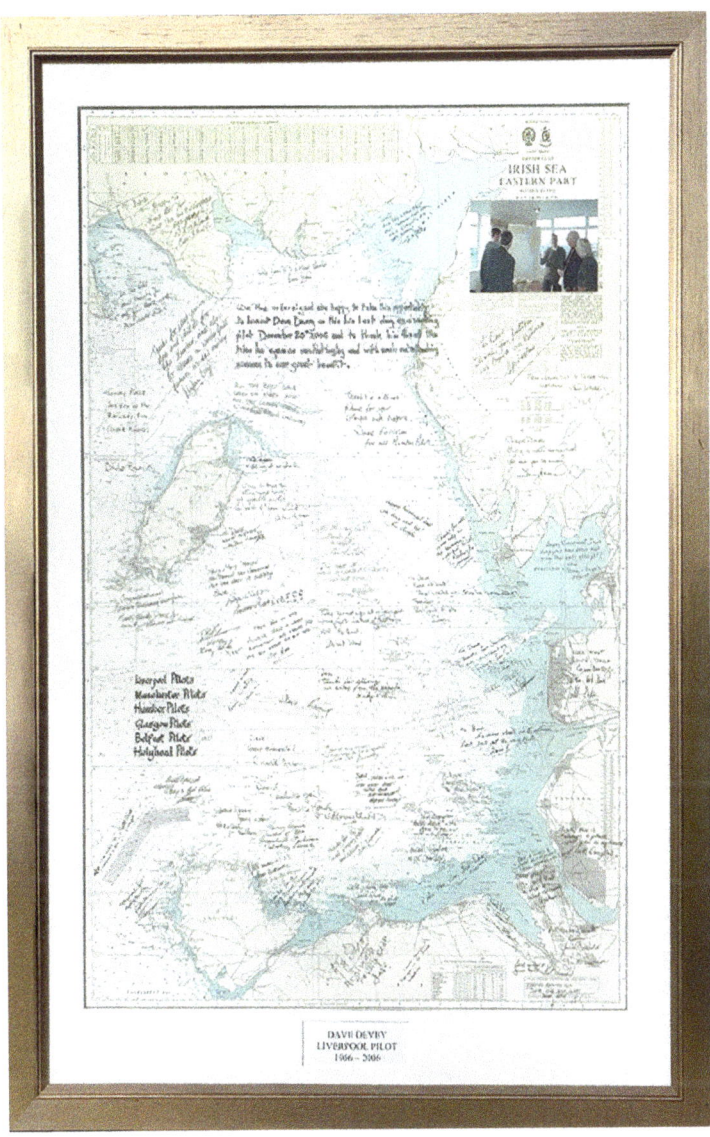

Admiralty Chart of the Liverpool Pilotage
District presented to David Devey on retirement in 2006.

My final appearance at the UKMPA conference held at the T&G centre in Bournemouth was one of nostalgia. On the one hand the presence of the representatives from Belfast who expressed their delight at their new-found freedom was particularly heartening but for me any joy I might have felt was offset by the absence of any representation from what used to be the largest pilot service in the UK, namely The Humber. I gave the conference an update of what was happening on Humberside with the hope that we would be able to challenge Associated British Ports (ABP) on the legality of their actions in dismissing 130 experienced pilots on the same day. Sadly, the case did not reach the law courts due to a lack of sufficient funds to cover the cost of the hearing. The loss of such a big player in the affairs of UK pilotage has left a permanent hole in the membership of the UKMPA from which I believe it has still not recovered.

My final farewell get together was at the pilots' annual hotpot in November 2007. To add to my delight, I was joined at table by two former Humber Pilots who had both lost their jobs as a result of the decision to employ pilots albeit illegally. One sat on my right, the other to my left. I had good company to talk about what went on and both told me that they had found good jobs which made me feel better. The pilots presented me with a most beautiful present in the shape of sailing pilot schooner number 10 crossing the bar in a strong gale of wind and entering the main channel at Q1 lighted buoy. It looked slightly odd as the first starboard-hand buoy was a bright red coloured can-shaped buoy. Today's buoyage system is the exact opposite of this and now has green-painted conical shaped buoys on the starboard side and red can buoys on the port side, which complies with international regulations that were brought in to standardise all navigational marks.

The Liverpool Pilot Service continued to prosper and moved out of the tally clerks hut and into a modern building where they were able to install a simulation centre for assisting in the training of their own pilots. Recruitment was once more in their own hands and they themselves could now decide how many pilots they needed to operate successfully whereas before they would be told by management how many they were permitted to have which was invariably on the low side in order to cut down the costs to the CHA. Duty rosters and leave periods were decided in house by the pilots as they were once more independent professional men and no longer employees reduced to a low-ranking position within the confines of harbour authority. It spelt an end to the numerous meetings between the reps and the harbour authority in an effort to improve the level of earnings only to be told at year's end that pilots cannot be treated any differently than other employee and would be given the same annual increase as everybody else which was usually less than inflation despite large annual increases in the revenue earned from pilotage. This money was kept by the harbour authority as the 1987 Pilotage Act allowed the CHAs to make a profit from pilotage. The newly accepted agreement calculated the percentage increase (or decrease) in the annual pilotage revenue figures compared to the previous year's figures and would then be applied to the annual uplift (or downturn) to the pilots' pool of earnings. The pilots would then distribute the agreed amount amongst the membership in shares dependant on the class of authorisation held. All of this procedure was enacted within the space of one annual meeting with the CHA which freed the representatives to spend the time saved on the business of piloting ships and not stuck in endless dialogue in meetings which produced very little in the way of progress.

Going back to my retirement, I was getting used to my new way of life with every night in my own bed and undisturbed by any phone calls alerting me to my next duty. Then it happened! On September 26th, 2007, a letter dropped onto my doormat telling me that I had been nominated for the Merchant Navy Medal and asked me if I would accept to allow my name to go forward. I was stunned by the news as I had been retired for almost a year. I nearly fell over myself in my haste to reply in case they changed their mind, and I flew off a "Yes I would be delighted" and sat back to wait for the answer. It came quickly back with a message that my name would be included in the list of awards together with details of the ceremony to be held in London in the church of Saint Michael Paternoster Royal which was home to the famous Lord Mayor Dick Whittington who is buried in the churchyard. The list of those nominated for the award was published in the London Gazette on October 22nd 2007and the date for the ceremony was fixed for December 5th with the medals to be presented by Admiral Lord West of Spithead who is the patron of The Mission to Seafarers whose headquarters are based at the church. The day went off smoothly and following the ceremony I, along with my two invited guests Terry Crowe and Andy Malcolm, who both played a major role in our fight for self-employment, all repaired post haste to the Old Bank of England in the company of our wives. You may wonder what possessed us to want to go to the Old Bank of England but when I tell you it is now a very beautiful pub that has been preserved just as it was when it was first built think you will understand our motives. A few celebratory pints and a train home was the perfect end to a very memorable day.

Dave Devey being presented the Merchant Navy Medal.

The fledgling pilot service continued to flourish and to go from strength to strength in its newly found freedom of independence. The year is 2012 and their adherence to safe practices in their everyday operations soon caught the attention of the leading maritime assessor namely Lloyds Register resulting in them being nominated for the top award by the International Standards for Pilotage Organisation which has its origins in the Port of Rotterdam. The award was presented to the Chairman of Liverpool Pilots by the Lord Mayor of Liverpool at a glittering ceremony held at The Town Hall which was attended by a number of dignitaries which included Louise Ellman MP for Liverpool Riverside who is Chairperson of the Transport Select Committee at Westminster and a delegation of Rotterdam Pilots, serving and retired Liverpool Pilots, of which I was one, and representatives from the Port Authority, Peel Ports. The award was endorsed by The Marine Accident Investigation Branch, which is a Government Department, who considers Liverpool to be " The most professional and forward thinking pilotage service in the UK".

Liverpool is the first UK pilotage service to win this prestigious award which reflects on the endeavours of the pilots as a body to view safety as being of paramount importance in the guidance of shipping in and out of the Mersey River. This is particularly relevant following the recent news that Liverpool will soon be hosting more and more large cruise liners following the approval of a boarding and landing facility at the Pierhead terminal. This award seems to fly in the face of government policy aimed at creating an all employed national pilotage service. Remember, as employees of the Mersey Docks and Harbour Company, the pilots lived in squalid accommodation, were downgraded to the level of foreman and were constantly attacked by the CHA to further reduce their numbers in order to save money which went into the CHAs coffers. How life has changed for the better in the short space of 6 years since leaving the employ of the MDHC.

In 2015 the pilots felt confident enough to suggest to the shipping company Cunard that an ideal way of celebrating their 175th anniversary would be to sanction the idea of bringing 3 of their most prestigious liners together on the same day to Liverpool namely Queen Elizabeth, Queen Mary and Queen Victoria. Cunard listened intently to the complex plan which had been drawn up by the pilots using the data gained from their own simulator. The plan showed each of the vessel's manoeuvres together with precise times when they would arrive at their designated places within the buoyed channel. It involved a highly co-ordinated operation in keeping with the maximum safety measures that needed to be observed in such a complex procedure. Each vessel would be allocated 2 pilots who would liaise with each of the other vessels throughout the exercise and perform a highly orchestrated programme which would result in all 3 "Queens" assembling in the river together and in sight of the original Cunard building at the Liverpool Pier Head. It resulted in a stunning display of perfectly performed and choreographed acts of pilotage by all six pilots who took part. A huge success which was witnessed by many thousands of onlookers who had gathered on each side of the river to watch the spectacle.

Queen Elizabeth, Queen Mary, and Queen Victoria
– Liverpool May 25th 2015.

I must stress the point that a pilotage service which operates under the yolk of the harbour authority would not be allowed the same scope to even think about doing such a thing let alone to organise the planning and execution of it themselves as happened in Liverpool that special day on May 25th, 2015. But the icing on the cake for the Liverpool Pilotage Service came in July 2016 when they were given admission to the Freedom Roll of Associations & Institutions of the City of Liverpool. The ceremony took place at the Liverpool Parish Church of Our Lady and Saint Nicholas which is situated near the waterfront and is the designated church for all seafarers who may be visiting the port. Following the church service, a reception was held at the Liverpool Town Hall in the presence of the Lord Mayor and other civic dignitaries to which I received an invitation. Sitting amongst my fellow pilots both active and retired I could not help but reflect on where we might have been today if we had not taken up the cudgels and fought the good fight to the finish. That gave me a great feeling of vindication for what we did in those dark days of employment in order to attain this position and a huge pride in what our present-day pilots are doing to uphold that unique status of independent professional men that befits the title of "Pilot".

It was important that the serving pilots should be made aware of the dangers of a return to the employment of the harbour authority and in particular to the ones who did not experience the humiliation felt by those who spent nine years of subjugation as a result of the decision to accept the offer of employment by the CHA in 1988. To this end

Terry Crowe suggested that we create a flag to commemorate the date on which we regained our status i.e. June 1st 1997. The flag that was created was comprised of a large Liver bird representing the city and port of Liverpool. This mythical bird has an olive branch in its beak representing peace and goodwill but also has very sharp talons which would be used to ward off any would-be attackers. This is the same bird that is perched on top of the Liver building at the Pier Head and legend has it that when a virgin passes underneath it flaps its wings. To date the bird has yet to flap its wings. The flag has the same bird standing on a plinth with the date 1997 and beneath that is the motto "Omnibus Aequalitas" which translated means "Everybody Equal" indicating the new constitution. All this is surmounted on a white and red flag which represents Pilotage.

Dave Devey with the Liverpool Pilots Independence flag.

A sea change in the UK government's approach towards Pilots needs to happen and happen soon. The government's reliance on the Harbourmasters Association to assist and advise them in developing legislation to control pilotage without any input from the pilots themselves is seriously misplaced. A number of the harbour masters are what we call "passed over pilots" which makes them envious of those who succeeded in being admitted into the fraternity. Coupled with a desire to exercise control over them, this has led to a civil servant adopting their stance to convert all UK Pilots into the employment of the harbour authority. Hence the disastrous outcome on the Humber. All done with a slight of hand in their interpretation of the 1987 Pilotage Act that supposedly allows them to force pilots into bondage "as a default option." This interpretation is totally misleading as the Act gives pilots the right to consider the CHAs OFFER of employment but following a ballot in favour of remaining self-employed the pilots can inform the CHA "that it need not do so". Nowhere in the act does it mention a "default option" but this crept into an advisory document entitled "The Port Marine Safety Code" which was created by the civil servant Andrew Burr.

As an island nation the UK needs to have a strong pilotage presence in order to cope with the 95 per cent of trade that uses shipping as a means of conveying goods which are vital to the country's survival. The catastrophic events which occurred on the Humber in 2002 following the simultaneous dismissal of all 130 self-employed pilots by the CHA on the grounds that employment, as the default option, would create a more efficient and safer service has proved to be a costly error which is still ongoing. Those people who were responsible for creating this mess including a certain civil servant have long since quit the scene of the disaster and left it to others to try to patch up the wreckage left behind. When compared to what has happened in Liverpool in a reverse situation it has only served to demonstrate that employment should never be considered as the default option.

Woodside Flag Hoisting - Dave Devey, Kevin Walsh, Jenny Crowe, Steve Watson and Terry Crowe.

Belfast Pilots Plaque dedicated to Maurice Cunningham and Dave Devey.

Jenny Crowe, Terry Crowe, Jean Devey and Dave Devey at Liverpool Town Hall at Freedom of the City of Liverpool Ceremony.

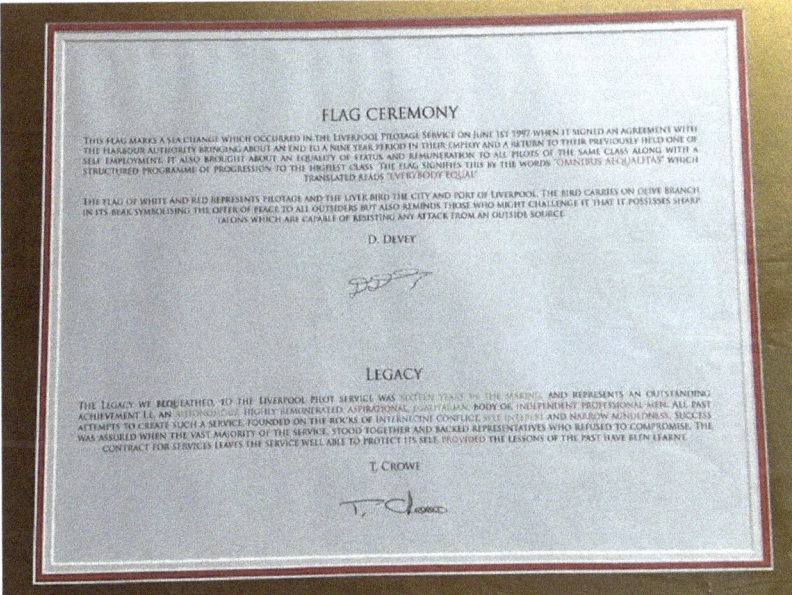

Flag ceremony.

Presentation of the Independence flag to the Liverpool Pilots.

Presentation of commemorative medals by the Liverpool Pilots to retired pilots D.Devey and T.E.Crowe in recognition of their outstanding leadership during the campaign in 1988 to 1997 to return the service to its time honoured status of Independence.

www.ingramcontent.com/pod-product-compliance
Lightning Source LLC
Chambersburg PA
CBHW041927090426
42743CB00021B/3465